Aebos 24.95

EVERYTHING YOU NEED TO KNOW

ATVs

STEVE CASPER

MOTORBOOKS

DEDICATION

To my Grandpa Chuck, who took me on my first trail rides in the bluffs and cow trails
along the mighty Mississippi River.

ACKNOWLEDMENTS

Thanks to the following for their help in putting this book together: Ray Sedorchuk, Jason Coffel,
Robert Jette, Glenn Hanson, Pat Carrigan, Dennis Cox, Doug Morris, Cain Smead, Joe Kosch, Mark Ansley,
Rusty Gilbert, James Phifer, Steve Hamilton, Lisa Cards, the National Off-Highway Vehicle Conservation
Council (NOHVCC), the All-Terrain Vehicle Association (ATVA), the ATV Safety Institute (ASI),
the Specialty Vehicle Institute of America (SVIA), Suzuki, Honda, Kawasaki, Yamaha, Polaris, Bombardier,
Arctic Cat, Cycle Country, Engelhart Center Motorsports (Madison, Wisconsin), and High-Lifter Products.

First published in 2005 by Motorbooks, an imprint of
MBI Publishing Company, Galtier Plaza, Suite 200,
380 Jackson Street, St. Paul, MN 55101-3885 USA

MBI Publishing Company titles are also available at
discounts in bulk quantity for industrial or sales-
promotional use. For details write to Special Sales
Manager at MBI Publishing Company, Galtier Plaza,
Suite 200, 380 Jackson Street, St. Paul,
MN 55101-3885 USA.

ISBN-13: 978-0-7603-2042-6
ISBN-10: 0-7603-2042-X

Editors: Lee Klancher and Leah Noel
Designer: Brenda C. Canales

Printed in China

On the front cover: The Kawasaki Brute Force 750
takes on some tough terrain. Hill-climbing with your
ATV has become an art form with the appearance of
ATVs that combine abundant power and torque
with independent rear suspension systems.
Pat Carrigan

On the frontispiece: Playing in the mud is part of
the fun with ATVs. Be sure and do so only in designated areas. *Lee Klancher*

On the title page: Part of the joys of ATVs is they
will take you into the backcountry that is otherwise
nearly inaccessible.

On the back cover: Sport quads are built for racing,
play riding, and tackling the dunes. *Pat Carrigan*

About the author:
Steve Casper has spent most of his motojournalism
career as an editor at *3&4 Wheel Action* and *Dirt
Wheels* magazines, producing over 230 issues since
1984. He has ridden ATVs in all corners of the
country and his racing resume includes motocross,
TT, cross country, desert, and ice events. In 2000,
Casper received the ATV Racing Legends Award in
the journalism category. Steve is currently the
communications director for the National Off-
Highway Vehicle Conservation Council and lives in
New Glarus, Wisconsin, with his wife and two
young daughters.

CONTENTS

Introduction

Over the last fifteen years, ATV riding has become one of the most popular outdoor recreation activities in the United States. Interest in the sport has grown because these vehicles can be used to do anything from mowing lawns to taking weekend trail riding adventures.

All-terrain vehicle—a name that pretty much says it all. These amazing and versatile machines are capable of tackling everything from nasty mud bogs and huge sand mountains to slushy snow and frozen lakes. They are as at home in the swamps of Louisiana as they are in the mountains of Colorado, the deserts of California, and the narrow, forested trails of Pennsylvania. Because they can traverse terrain like no other off-highway vehicle, they have become both valuable working vehicles as well as extremely popular recreational machines.

Yet very few folks could have ever imagined just how popular ATVs would become. In the first years of this century, annual sales of ATVs topped the one million-unit mark, outselling dirt and street motorcycles combined! The incredible appeal goes beyond these vehicles' capabilities, though. Unlike dirt bikes that require a certain amount of athletic ability to master, ATVs possess a relatively easy learning curve. And when compared to dirt bikes and snowmobiles, all-terrain vehicles are much more suitable for year-round use. On top of that, the age and gender of aspiring ATV riders pose few limitations, as there are many different-sized models to choose from. In fact, one of the least-known aspects of ATVing in America is the popularity of these four-wheeled machines with physically challenged riders.

The "work and play" aspect of ATVs is also quite unique among off-highway vehicles. The same machine that you use to cruise down the trails for a Sunday afternoon ride may be recruited the next day for lawn mowing or hauling rocks. In fact, the number of workhorse tasks an ATV can be used for is nearly endless. ATV accessory catalogs are jam-packed with snowplows, winches, lawn mowers, seed spreaders, and dozens of other farming implements. Farmers and ranchers throughout the country find ATVs especially useful and a lot less expensive to own and operate than a tractor, and several ATV manufacturers even feature "specialty" packages that completely outfit an ATV for specific purposes such as ranching, camping, or hunting.

The full spectrum of the recreational end of ATVing is nearly as diverse as the utility aspect. There are those riders who prefer relatively easy, smooth trails for a casual day of sightseeing and camaraderie with their friends and family. And then there are others who enjoy the exhilaration of going fast down bumpy, twisty trails, occasionally stopping to tackle a tough hillclimb. At the pinnacle of the sporting aspect of ATVing are the riders who choose to lay it all on the line at an organized racing event. Depending on where you live, there are many different forms of competitions to choose from, each with a wide variety of classes for different ages and abilities.

ATVs have taken on a social aspect as well. Local clubs have sprung up all over the country, typically holding organized rides and special events every month. The biggest rage as we head into the new century is the many ATV festivals, jamborees, and mud runs. These events keep drawing more and more folks every year, many of who base their family vacation around riding ATVs.

Government agencies have also embraced the usefulness of ATVs. The most noticeable are search and rescue crews who are dispatched on ATVs whenever an outdoor enthusiast runs into trouble in the rugged backcountry. Police, sheriffs, lifeguards, fish and game officers, and land agencies such as the Forest Service and the Bureau of Land Management also utilize ATVs. Even scientists have discovered what a valuable tool ATVs can be for their studies out in the bush.

Basically, all ATV riders strive to have a fun, safe, and fulfilling experience with their machines. They've invested quite a bit in the initial purchase and want their all-terrain vehicle to be reliable and work to its peak performance, whether that means riding for sport or doing work. In the following chapters, you'll learn about nearly every aspect of the ATV world. First you'll learn how to pick the right machine and riding gear, how to gain the basic riding skills, and once that is accomplished, how to conquer the more advanced track and trail techniques.

For the gearheads (and yes, there a lot in the ATV world), this book will offer up a ton of information on how to modify your quad for specific applications and the importance of keeping a proper maintenance schedule. There's also a chapter on what to do when your ATV won't start. Other information covered includes how to prepare for the various types of organized ATV

competition offered in America, how to find places to ride, and how to start an ATV club.

On a final note, the text often will refer to ATVs by different names, as owners in different parts of the country refer to these vehicles as wheelers, four-wheelers, ATVs, and quads. I'll use these same terms as well, and sometimes I'll simply refer to them as machines. No matter what they're called, I hope you enjoy *ATVs: Everything You Need to Know* and get lots of good information from it. But above all, have fun and welcome to the wonderful world of ATVing!

Whether they're used in ranching, farming, or landscaping a large lot, utility quads have become one the fast-growing segments of the ATV market.

Taking a day or week trek on your quad is one way you can get to see vistas like this, without having to spend hours hiking through rugged terrain.

HOW TO CHOOSE THE RIGHT ATV
FINDING THE PERFECT FOUR-WHEELER FOR YOU

Chapter 1

HERE WE WILL COVER

- Types of ATVs

- Engines, transmissions, and drives

- Suspension systems and brakes

- 2WD vs. 4WD and differentials

- Buying or selling a used quad

The Suzuki Ozark 250 is a good example of a smaller, less expensive sport/utility ATV, one of the most popular kinds of ATVs on the market. This quad is fun and easy to ride on the trails, but its two-wheel drive and small engine limit its capabilities in mud bogs and more extreme terrain.

Since today's four-wheelers generally have good long-term durability, they will last several years, again making you want to avoid any sort of impulsive buy.

The best news for potential ATV buyers is that today there are more ATV choices than ever before, which means you can get the perfect machine for your riding style and intended use. However, the number of choices does make whittling down your options more difficult.

Buying an ATV is a big investment and shouldn't be taken lightly. Since today's four-wheelers generally have good long-term durability, they will last several years, again making you want to avoid any sort of impulsive buy.

Fortunately, with a little bit of research on your part, you can go into any dealership fully armed with the info you need to make the right choice when buying a new quad. Your ultimate goal should be to buy a machine that not only fits you just right and is easy for you to ride, but also has plenty of power for your needs, a comfortable suspension system, the appropriate "thrill factor", and all the features you'll need for getting any chores done.

To make things easier for both the dealers and the buyers, the manufacturers have designated certain categories, or classifications, of ATVs. Most of models fit neatly into one category or another, although there are many models that cross over into more than one classification because of certain features. In fact, the lines between some of the categories have begun to blur in the last decade as nearly all of the manufacturers have designed their utility models with considerably more performance for those riders who want to get the complete ATV experience (work and play) from one machine.

YOUTH MODELS
The youth, or mini, classification has recently been one of the fastest-growing segments in the ATV world. Youth four-wheelers are basically smaller, lighter, and less-expensive versions of the adult models. Nearly all of them are designed for play and recreational trail riding with the family, yet some of the models can be quite competitive in the youth division racing in basically stock form.

In this category, there are a number of lesser-known brands that offer mini machines, many of them designed and built in foreign countries. As a result, the price range and difference in quality of the youth models tends to vary more than the other categories. Engine sizes range from 50cc to 125cc (there's a lot more two-strokes found here than in other categories) and most feature an automatic transmission.

ENTRY-LEVEL FOUR-WHEELERS

This class is the next step up from youth models as far as size and price go. Some manufacturers and enthusiast magazines also like to call this category the Recreational Trail Class. These machines are designed to be easy to ride with fairly tame handling manners and powerplants. The engines are typically no-frills, air-cooled four-strokes that range from 125cc to 250cc. Some of these machines feature automatic transmissions while others require shifting, but no clutch to operate. All of the full-sized quads built today, including all the ATVs in this class, have some sort of suspension system both front and rear.

Like the title of this classification states, these machines are a great starting point for folks who have never ridden off-road vehicles before. Another group of riders that prefer four-wheelers from this class are those who are physically smaller than the typical adult rider and/or riders who prefer to keep their speed at a casual pace. Yet tough trail situations, such as overcoming big mud bogs or boulder fields, quickly tax these machines beyond their limits.

UTILITY QUADS

Utility ATVs are by definition designed primarily for heavy-duty work, such as hauling cargo on the front and rear racks, pulling a trailer or farm implement, or pushing a plow blade. That's why these machines have become so popular among people who own large amounts of land, run their own ranch, or farm their land.

A number of industries and law enforcement officers, land managers, scientists, and rescue personnel use this type of ATV. Utility four-wheelers have also been a favorite of hunters, campers, and fisherman ever since their inception in the mid-1980s.

For much of their history, utility quads have typically been regarded as sluggish-handling behemoths with slow, but powerful, engines and a limited amount of suspension travel. But that has changed over the years. Today utility four-wheelers are built to be fun and comfortable on the trails. When the going gets rough in the mud, rocks, or steep hillclimbs, modern utility quads typically come through like champs. They have a high ground clearance and get great traction.

Some utility ATV models feature four-wheel drive, while others get by with two-wheel

The Honda Sportrax 300 features a manual five-speed transmission, disc brakes, electric start, and a reverse gear. It is solidly placed in the sport quad category and loves to jump, slide, and pop wheelies.

TIP

LISTEN TO YOUR PALS ABOUT UNRELIABLE BRANDS

When ATV magazines do their evaluations of most models, they rarely have a chance to put a lot of miles on the machines to see how well they hold up in the long run. However, there are some folks who do have a good feel for which quad brands are durable and dependable, and that's a riding group or club.

If several of them have had bad experiences with certain models or brands, pay attention to what they're saying since they generally know what they're talking about. And keep in mind that some quads that may break down quite frequently in, say, muddy conditions may run just fine for many years in the desert if all their troubles were caused by water and mud.

The Rincon 650 is Honda's top-of-the-line sport/utility 4x4 vehicle. It features a unique liquid-cooled, four-valve, dual-pushrod longitudinally mounted engine, and the transmission can be used in either a fully automatic or manual shift mode.

drive. And in many cases, the exact same model can be purchased in either version (with the price difference typically being around $1,000). There also are dozens of extra features that can be found on utility quads, such as storage boxes, auxiliary electrical outlets, removable headlights, independent rear suspension, and liquid-cooled engines. Four-stroke engines ranging in size from 250cc to 700cc power most utility quads.

SPORT/UTILITY ATVS

The sport/utility category has probably done more than any other to increase the popularity of four-wheelers. These machines combine the working capabilities of utility quads with the sporting characteristics of the performance and racing ATVs, so ATVs are no longer strictly one or the other. Because of their flexibility, these machines are offered in a wide array of models offered year after year, and often are the best sellers.

Sport/utility quads can basically be looked at in two different ways: You can describe them as sport machines with racks, a trailer hitch, and 4WD or you could say they're utility quads with faster engines and longer travel suspension. In fact, when you look under the skin of many of these sport/utility ATVs, you'll find that the manufacturers actually based their original designs for these quads on already existing sport or utility models.

The best part of these machines is that you literally can spend the morning mowing the lawn with your quad and then take the same machine out for a fast afternoon trail ride, tackling jumps and churning out big broadslides. Sport/utility four-wheelers are generally very easy to ride and are a great choice for novice trail riders. They can also tackle the tough stuff like mud bogs and hillclimbs just as well as the utility quads can.

Most feature completely automatic transmissions and floorboards rather than footpegs and they also come in both 2WD and 4WD. They have four-stroke engines ranging from 250cc to 800cc (and up, depending on where ATVs evolve in the future).

SPORT QUADS

The machines that fit into this category were built with one goal in mind: fun! Sport ATVs typically feature peppy engines, long-travel suspension, a relatively light overall weight, and great handling for both the track and trail. Sport four-wheelers are great at jumping, hitting the rough stuff, sliding around corners, and popping wheelies. Experienced riders can fly down the trails at a quick pace that keeps them on their toes and gives them plenty of exercise.

Sport quads also have a racier look to them when compared to utility or sport/utility ATVs. In fact, modified sport quads are popular in the beginner classes at motocross and TT races and can be raced nearly stock in cross-country events.

Most sport four-wheelers rely on a five-speed transmission with a manual hand-controlled clutch. This makes them more challenging to ride than the auto-tranny models, but in the long run the shifting skills you'll learn riding them will come in quite handy if you ever want to go racing or step up to a machine in the high-performance category. With just a few exceptions, four-stroke engines ranging in size from 200cc to 400cc power almost all sport ATVs.

ANECDOTE

CONSIDER YOUR DEALER

After buying my first ATV, I was pretty much stuck going to the one dealer in my small town that carried parts for the brand I bought. Even after several years of going into their shop, I still didn't like their attitude. On the other hand, I got along just fine with the folks who work at the only other dealership in town and at times I wished I had bought one of their brands instead.

Of course, one shouldn't buy one brand or another based on how well you happen to like the dealership, but it is something to consider.

HIGH-PERFORMANCE ATVS

High-performance quads are the Corvettes and Ferraris of the ATV world. They're designed to accelerate the fastest, jump the highest, and broad slide the longest. Whether you're in the sand dunes, woods, or desert, there's nothing that can blaze down a rough trail like one of these race-bred machines. They've got fast, water-cooled powerplants with either five- or six-speed manual transmissions and the longest travel shocks of any class. Race-like handling is the goal of every manufacturer in this highly competitive class where the overall performance of each machine is reported in detail by the enthusiast magazines (as well as their current standings on the racetracks throughout the country).

In the late 1980s, two-stroke engines powered virtually every high-performance four-wheeler offered. That has changed entirely as high-tech four-stroke engines, many of which are patterned after their dirt bike counterparts, now dominate the class. Engine sizes currently range from 350cc to a whopping twin-cylinder 700cc monster. To win at the top levels in racing, a rider pretty much has to utilize a high-performance quad.

Though high-performance ATVs work great on the trail, they do have some downfalls, such as lower ground clearance and subpar mud bog and boulder capabilities.

Most of the quads in this class are harder to ride due to their manual gearboxes and clutch and their high-strung engines. And although the suspension can take some huge hits, the tighter-wound high-performance ATVs generally don't deliver the same comfortable ride on the trails that say a sport/utility quad might. In fact, when a high-performance quad is ridden to its full potential, the operator usually isn't even sitting down!

TWO-RIDER VEHICLES

This is the newest ATV classification, which appeared on the scene in 2002. When Canadian manufacturer Bombardier first introduced this type of ATV, many industry watchers were unnerved by it. They were nervous about the safety factor, as before this time riders had always been discouraged from carrying passengers on their quads. But even with warnings, many riders throughout the country regularly rode trails two-up.

At least Bombardier's machine was built for two, so riders no longer had to share a single seat and set of footpegs. So was Arctic Cat's follow-up machine. In fact, both machines had similar features: a slightly longer wheelbase for added stability, a second, slightly raised seat with grab bars for the passenger, and a second set of floorboard/footpegs.

Some utility ATVs like this Polaris feature "dump beds," which come in real handy for construction workers, ranchers, and farmers. Other features found on many utility ATVs include accessory electrical plugs, removable headlamps, waterproof storage containers, and full dashboards.

In the late 1980s, two-stroke engines powered virtually every high-performance four-wheeler offered. That has changed entirely as high-tech four-stroke engines, many of which are patterned after their dirt bike counterparts, now dominate the class.

More sport/utility machines are sold than any other type of ATV. Why? Because they're fun and easy to ride on the trails, yet they still retain racks and other utility features for chore time.

ALERT!

WHAT'S THE WORD ON ENGINE BREAK-IN TIME?

There are lots of opinions regarding the break-in period of an ATV engine. Some will argue to baby the engine for the first few rides, while others claim you should run it as hard as you can. The safe bet is somewhere in between.

The thing you don't want to do during break-in is run the engine at the same rpm for an extended period of time. Vary the throttle, but avoid full-throttle runs and hard starts and hard stops. Make sure during your first rides that the engine is good and warmed up before riding. After breaking it in, hitting the throttle hard on a cold engine is still a bad idea.

So far the concept seems to be working out quite well, but operators of these machines should always keep their speeds at a relatively casual pace.

ENGINE TYPES: TWO- OR FOUR-STROKES

During the mid- to late-1980s, ATV buyers had a big decision to make when it came to engines: Did they want a two-stroke or a four-stroke engine to power their new quad? Two-stroke engines offer a better horsepower-to-weight ratio over a four-stroke. The same goes for displacement—a 250cc two-stroke will churn out quite a bit more horsepower than a 250cc four-stroke.

However, two-stroke engines require oil to be mixed in with the gas, and they smoke and pollute the air more than a four-stroke. In addition, four-strokes get considerably better gas mileage than a two-stroke.

As the popularity of the racing models waned in the early 1990s, so did the number of two-stroke-powered quads. That fact, coupled with pressures from the California Air Resources Board (CARB) regarding off-highway vehicle (OHV) emissions in the Golden State, resulted in the steady elimination of virtually every two-stroke–powered four-

wheeler. By the time the new century rolled around, only a handful of two-stroke–powered adult-sized ATVs remained.

So for most potential ATV purchasers today, the question of whether to choose a quad powered by either a two- or four-stroke engine is moot. Unless you've got your heart set on the very unique Yamaha Banshee 350 or Blaster 200 (models which have changed little from the late 1980s), or a Gas Gas Wild 300, you'll be buying a four-stroke. Yet you'll still have plenty of options as to what kind and size of four-stroke engine you want on your quad.

AIR-COOLED AND LIQUID-COOLED ENGINES

To keep engines from overheating, air-cooled powerplants rely on the simple and age-old method of having external cooling fins built right on to the cylinder. The engines are usually positioned in the ATV so that as much air as possible flows over the cooling fins while the quad is in motion.

Liquid-cooled systems (also known as water-cooled, even though the coolant is actually a mixture of anti-freeze and water) are considerably more efficient at keeping the engine temperatures down, though. The system works by flowing the liquid coolant from a radiator mounted on the frame to the hollow channels surrounding the cylinder. It's pretty much the same setup that you'll find in your passenger car. Many ATVs also have an auxiliary fan that blows on the radiator to further cooling. The fan comes in really handy when the quad is traveling at slow speeds, such as during lawn mowing or farm implement work.

A cooler-running engine is better in several ways. One is that power delivery stays consistent and strong; another is that the overall life of the engine is increased, as well as the timespan between overhauls. Overheated engines strain parts and decrease the effectiveness of the engine lubricants. Also, a hot ATV engine can be quite a nuisance for the rider, especially when your quad radiates heat right onto your legs.

But there is one factor that helps the efficiency of the air-cooled units: Some air-cooled ATVs feature external oil coolers that also help keep engine temperatures down, and some of these oil coolers also have fans.

ELECTRONIC FUEL INJECTION

Many utility and sport/utility quads now feature electronic fuel injection (EFI). These systems are very similar to what is found in your passenger car. One of the most noticeable advantages of EFI is that there is no manual choke to hassle with (and forget to turn off!). This eliminates troublesome starting in very cold weather or when the engine is overheated. The way EFI works is that a computer chip responds to sensors that tell the system how much fuel to send

into the carburetor. This allows the ATV's engine to work to its full potential even when there are drastic changes in elevation or temperature.

Conventionally aspirated ATVs suffer a noticeable power loss when riding in the mountains, but that is no longer a concern with a quad that features EFI. There are even more advantages to EFI because the engine works much more efficiently, meaning better fuel mileage and less pollution. Chances are good that more and more ATV models will be showing up at the dealers with electronic fuel injection.

The high-performance end of ATVing got a big boost when Yamaha introduced the Raptor 660R in the late 1990s. From there, many other manufacturers came up with their own versions of big-bore four-stroke fun machines.

American-made Polaris ATVs have been trendsetters for the past couple of decades. Polaris was the first company to utilize completely automatic transmissions and floorboards rather than footpegs. Most of the other manufacturers of utility and sport/utility machines have followed suit.

French-Canadian manufacturer Bombardier jumped into the ATV world in the mid-90s and has designed many innovative machines. This interesting-looking DS 650 high-performance model is a favorite of dune riders and long-distance racers.

The majority of four-wheelers sold today feature completely automatic transmissions. They are literally as simple as driving a passenger car.

SINGLE CYLINDERS AND TWIN CYLINDERS

Single-cylinder engines power the overwhelming majority of four-wheelers available today, but twin-cylinder quads are making their presence known in the ATV world. The first twin-cylinder quad was the Kawasaki Prairie 650, which came out as a 2002 model.

The advantage of a twin-cylinder motor is that it provides more power over a single cylinder of the same displacement. They also rev quicker than a single. However, twin-cylinder engines are considerably bigger and heavier, and they are a challenge to package into an ATV. Fuel tanks need to be moved beneath the seat, switching places with the air intake, which then resides in front of the rider.

AUTOMATIC AND MANUAL TRANSMISSIONS

The majority of four-wheelers sold today feature completely automatic transmissions. They are literally as simple as driving a passenger car. Most consist of a variable clutch, belt-drive system similar to that found on snowmobiles. However, some of the manufacturers have gone in a different direction with their auto transmissions by designing complex, internal gear-driven systems. The gear-driven systems are a bit heavier and more expensive to make, but are also more reliable and won't get flooded during deepwater crossings. Belt-drives also emit quite a bit of heat in the summer.

The two kinds of manual transmissions used in modern quads are the traditional five-

Kawasaki's Brute Force 750 4x4 is great example of a fast and fun sport/utility ATV. It features a twin-cylinder four-stroke engine, independent rear suspension, front-locking differential, and a fully automatic transmission with engine braking.

or six-speed with a manual clutch or a system with an automatic clutch. The manual clutch is used on virtually all racing ATVs and dirt bikes. With this clutch, you shift with your left foot while your left hand controls the clutch; the advantage is that you can precisely control engine rpm and traction. It takes some skill to really do this, but it's the reason why expert trail riders and racers prefer this setup to an auto tranny.

With the automatic clutch setup, you can shift through the gears with your left foot, without worrying about using the clutch, making this system a popular choice with entry level and utility ATV riders.

To further complicate matters, ATVs that have manual shifters can have different kinds of shift systems. There is the standard left-foot shifter that is by far the most common. The other type is push-button shift

Suzuki's little QuadSport Z250 provides a fun and challenging ride for smaller or younger sport riders. It features sharp looks, a manual-clutch, five-speed transmission (with reverse), shaft-drive, and six inches of wheel travel in the front and seven inches in the rear.

Bombardier was the first manufacturer to design an ATV for two riders, but since then several other makers have introduced similar models. Two-up machines generally have longer wheelbases, beefed-up suspension systems, and an extra seat and set of footpegs. It is strongly advised that no more than one person ride a conventional ATV since carrying the extra person affects the handling of the machine.

A sport/utility model like the Bombardier Outlander 4x4 works best while tackling tough terrain like this. Sport and high-performance machines are certainly fun on the trails, but when you get into slow-going situations, their handling and engine characteristics can be a bit of a handful.

where the gears are changed by the rider's thumb with a toggle-like switch on the handlebar. And then there are two different types of these: mechanical and electronic thumb shifters.

As a final note, at least one quad (at the time of this book's writing) features both an automatic transmission and a multi-speed manual transmission, where the operator can switch back and forth from one to the other.

FINAL DRIVE: CHAIN AND SHAFT

Chain-drive ATV systems have two advantages over shaft-drives—they're lighter and less expensive to make. You can also change overall gear ratios quite easily by changing either the front or rear sprocket, but that's usually only a concern for racers.

However, chain drives require more maintenance (chain tightening and chain and sprocket replacement) and decrease ground clearance. As a result, they are especially vulnerable in extreme muddy or rocky conditions.

Shaft-driven quads require little or no maintenance to the final drive system. Almost all current 4WD quads have shaft-drive front and rear, as do most of the sport/utility wheelers. The majority of sport and high-performance quads utilize chain drive.

REAR SUSPENSION SYSTEMS

ATV rear suspension systems can basically be broken down into two primary categories: single-shock, swingarm-style with a straight axle and completely independent with single or double A-arms.

There are currently lots of choices in the kids-size ATV class, like this Yamaha Raptor 80. Even though the Raptor is a four-stroke, this is one of the few types of ATVs where you can still find a variety of machines powered by two-stroke engines.

The independent system is typically referred to as IRS (independent rear suspension). A generalization is that most sport and high-performance quads utilize a swingarm and straight axle while most utility and sport/utility ATVs have IRS, although there are exceptions to both. Very few of the kid quads and budget-minded entry-level machines feature IRS (which adds weight and cost to the vehicle).

With IRS, each rear wheel moves independently of the other, just like in the front. When traversing big ruts, rocks, and other obstacles, the IRS system keeps the quad more level and stable than if it had a straight axle. While blazing down the trail, the

While certain colors are associated with certain manufacturers (Yamaha blue, Suzuki yellow, Kawasaki green, Honda red, etc.), there is some interesting crossover at times. This special edition of the popular Yamaha YFZ450 is one of them. The YFZ has been one of the most successful ATVs on the nation's racetracks throughout the early part of this century.

Bombardier's Traxter 500XL certainly has the look of a tough workhorse. It features a two-valve pushrod engine, a dump bed, a rear-mounted radiator, and the exclusive Bombardier step-through seating design.

ALERT!

BEWARE OF DEALS TOO GOOD TO BE TRUE

All-terrain vehicles are not cheap. However, with the recent influx of dozens of "off-brand" four-wheelers, some of the price tags on new quads have dropped to enticing levels. Most of these low-priced machines are copies of models from the established manufacturers. And most of these copies are mini quads or small-motored two-wheel drives.

The quality of some of these quads is quite questionable and the old adage "you get what you pay for" may apply. It's especially tough when something breaks and the company doesn't back it up or the replacement parts are hard to find.

IRS quad almost always delivers a smoother ride. The downside is that an IRS quad loses some of its finesse in the corners since the quad tends to lean over on the outside rear wheel (most IRS quads have an anti-sway bar installed in the back to lessen this effect).

Racing, sport, and high-performance quads tend to stick with the conventional straight axle for handling, weight, and cost reasons. You can charge into a corner much harder with a straight axle, which is a must for these types of machines. However, at least one manufacturer (Polaris) is offering a high-performance machine with IRS.

Another type of rear suspension currently on the market is a twin-shock, swing-axle setup. Although the axle is solid, it can pivot up and down with each rear wheel,

giving a semi-IRS performance. There are also straight axle, swingarm arrangements with dual shocks, which is primarily an engineering option to get the engine and air box to all fit neatly under the quad. The performance with this option is similar to other straight axle machines.

DISC AND DRUM BRAKES

Most quads today feature the superior disc brake systems. Simply put, they stop better, last longer, and work much better in muddy and wet conditions. In the winter, you won't have any problems with discs freezing up while drum brakes can get water inside that freezes after you put the machine away. In the early days of ATVing only the high-performance machines sported disc brakes,

If your forte is jumping high and going fast, you should consider a high-performance ATV like the Honda Sportrax 450R. With a powerful, quick-revving four-stroke engine, manual five-speed transmission, long-travel suspension, and disc brakes, your buddies will be hard-pressed to keep up!

but now many of the utility and sport/utility machines do so as well. For more on disc and drum brake maintenance, see Chapter 12.

TWO-WHEEL DRIVE AND FOUR-WHEEL DRIVE

A big question many ATV buyers have is whether to get a two-wheel or four-wheel drive. It basically comes down to how extreme the terrain is that you'll be using it in. Four-wheel drive quads can do a much better job getting through muddy sections, climbing steep hills, crawling over big obstacles—such as logs and rocks—and navigating deep water holes. Four-wheel-drive ATVs can also plow more snow, carry more cargo, and pull bigger farm implements and trailers.

Nearly every four-wheel-drive ATV has a button that allows the operator to switch back and forth from two- to four-wheel drive "on the fly" (though the manufacturers recommend slowing down before making the switch). Some ATV four-wheel drive systems

have sensors that automatically switch the ATV to the four-wheel-drive mode when it feels the need for front-wheel drive. As we mentioned earlier, many ATV models come in

North American manufacturer Arctic Cat now offers a complete lineup of sport, utility, sport/utility, and youth ATVs. Their sales of ATVs have in fact surpassed their snowmobile sales for most of this century.

TIP

IS THERE A BACKUP PULLSTART?

With nearly all of the four-wheelers made today featuring a push-button, electric starting system, you're in quite a jam if the battery goes dead . . . or are you? Most ATVs have a backup pull starter somewhere on the side of the engine. Some models don't, so if you plan on doing a lot of riding by yourself (not necessarily the safest thing to do in the first place), you may want to make sure your new quad has a backup pull start.

All-terrain vehicles have opened up a whole new world of outdoor exploration for people with physical handicaps. The quads with the easiest-to-use features, such as automatic transmissions, single-lever brakes, reverse gear, and electric start, work best.

BUYING OR SELLING A USED ATV
GOOD DEALS TO BE HAD BOTH WAYS

Buying a used four-wheeler can save you a lot of dough. However, given the nature of off-road riding, many used ATVs will have taken quite a beating before they show up in the classifieds or on eBay.

With that in mind, always figure out how much you'll need to spend to get a used ATV running in good, reliable condition. Take the following checklist with you when you go to take a look at a used machine.

1. Raise the ATV up with the help of a friend and stand it on the rear grab bar (remember to turn off the gas first). This will allow you to inspect the undercarriage for any serious dents or damage.

2. Look closely at the frame, especially the shock mounts, A-arm mounts, and intersections of frame components for any signs of rust. Here you may see signs of a stress crack that require welding and repainting.

3. On 4x4 ATVs, inspect the CV joint boots. They should be in excellent condition. Any crack or tears will allow water and dirt to enter and could cause costly repairs.

4. Also on 4x4 ATVs, if possible, remove the front and rear differential inspection plugs. If the gear lube looks like chocolate milk, the oil is contaminated with water and there could be damage to the bearings.

5. Check the ATV's engine oil to see whether it looks contaminated.

6. Shine a flashlight into the gas tank and look for rust. Yes, a gas tank can rust, and rust can cause carburetor problems.

7. Raise the ATV and support the front of it with jack stands. Then try to move each front wheel in and out from top to bottom and side to side to check for worn wheel bearings and ball joints. Do the same for the rear.

8. With the ATV on the ground, move the handlebars back and forth. This will identify worn tie rod ends.

9. Remove the seat and take the air box lid off. An air box can collect water and damage an engine.

10. Check all headlights, taillights, the engine shutoff switch, and key switch. Check that the lights and gauges on the dash work.

11. Check the hand, foot, and parking brakes. Do they operate smoothly or stick? Check for damaged or cracked cables.

12. Check the exhaust. Is there oil dripping out of it? Has the spark arrestor been removed? Almost every state and national forest requires that you have one.

13. Check for worn-out tires or tires full of plugs. These really aren't a problem, but worn tires or plugs should be a negotiating point on price.

14. Look closely at the front or rear sprockets. Each point should be uniform. If they are worn more on one side or have a hooked appearance, a new chain and sprocket set is in order.

15. How easily does the ATV start? Any hesitation in starting could be as simple as a carburetor out of adjustment or a dirty carb that needs cleaning or a worn out spark plug, a clogged air filter, or something more serious. You should also pay attention to if you see any noticeable smoke appears when the engine starts or if there is excessive smoke as you apply more throttle.

16. Take a test ride. Check how smoothly the ATV starts to move; a hesitation or jerking here could mean big problems. Whether it's an automatic or manual transmission, check how well it shifts into the various gear or drive modes. Do the handlebars turn easily left and right? If the engine speed increases while turning, the cables could be routed improperly. Also, smoothly apply each of the hand and foot breaks separately. Do they make a horrible sound, and are they effective? It could be more than just brake pads. The drums or rotors could be badly worn or scored beyond safe use.

17. After you buy a used machine, it's a good idea to change all the fluids so that you know you have fresh oil, etc.

SELLING POINTS
You can take several tips from the checklist above as to how to prepare your used quad for sale as well as some of the others listed below.

• Clean the air filter and air box and change the engine oil. If you have a shaft drive, change the oil in the drive unit and transfer case.

• Make sure the battery is charged and the engine starts easily. Put fresh gas in the tank if the ATV has been sitting awhile. If the muffler needs repacking, do it to keep noise and excess smoke down.

• If the racks or parts of the frame are badly scratched and rusted, spot-sand them down and give those areas a quick and easy spray paint job.

• The condition of the plastic fenders says a lot to a potential buyer. An all-new set of plastic is pretty expensive, so you probably won't want to go that route. However, plastic repair kits are available, which can fix tears and rips. A final coat of Armor-All after cleaning can really jazz things up. You may also want to remove any stickers you've added.

• Check that all the wheels are moving easily and aren't bent. Bent handlebars aren't too cool either, so see what you can do to get them as straight as possible. Replacement sets can be had for under $20.

• Lube the cables so all the controls are running smoothly. Grease any zerk fittings to keep squeaks down during a test ride.

• Torn seats look pretty bad. There are repair kits to fix them up without having to buy a new one.

either two- or four-wheel drive with the price difference being around $1,000. And of course, the four-wheel-drive machines will also be heavier.

LIMITED-SLIP DIFFERENTIALS, TORQUE-SENSING DIFFERENTIALS, AND DIFFERENTIAL LOCK
Almost all four-wheel-drive quads feature a limited-slip front differential that shares the power with the wheel that needs it the most

(the one that is getting traction), rather than having the wheel that is slipping (up in the air perhaps), spinning wildly like it would on a machine with an "open" differential. One step above limited-slip is torque-sensing differential, which does an even better job of getting power to the wheel getting the most traction.

A feature you may see on a four-wheel drive quad in combination with either of the two differentials described above is a front differential lock. This is used when the rider is

Many utility and sport/utility quads now feature completely independent rear suspension (IRS) systems that provide a smother, more stable ride over really rough terrain. However, IRS also adds to the cost and weight of the machine as well as making it tougher to slide around corners.

in a situation where he or she may be getting stuck, usually in deep thick mud. To engage the differential lock, most models have a small lever on the handlebars to progressively "lock" the two front wheels and give them both full power to get out of the situation. So

if a locked front end is the best for extreme terrain, why not always leave it locked? Well, the steering gets extremely difficult, which is why most four-wheel drives spend most of their time being operated in the limited-slip or torque-sensing mode.

The Yamaha Grizzly sport/utility machine has been a favorite of southern state mud boggers for years. It utilizes the same 660cc four-stroke powerplant that is found in the Raptor 660R sport machine.

RIDING GEAR
FOR PROTECTION AND COMFORT

HERE WE WILL COVER

- **Helmets and goggles**
- **Riding boots**
- **Gloves**
- **Jerseys and pants**
- **What do you really need?**
- **Gear care and cost**

To think there's no chance you'll ever have an accident while trail riding is about the same as thinking you could never be in a car accident. You wear your seatbelt, right? Well, make sure you wear your safety gear whenever you go riding!

Most ATV riders always wear at least a helmet, goggles, gloves, and boots whenever they go riding. These basic items, along with a jersey and riding pants, not only offer greater protection than "civilian" clothes, but also make riding much more comfortable.

The protection concept behind this gear is two-fold. First, riding gear protects you from the elements—including branches, bugs, mud, dust, and roost that may come your way. Secondly, riding gear protects you if you fall off or crash your ATV. This is when you're really glad you have all your safety gear on.

As an extra bonus, a full set of durable riding gear also eliminates the surprising wear and tear that ATV riding does to street clothes and tennis shoes. And when it comes to riding in cold and wet weather, the modern "enduro" riding jackets do an incredible job of keeping you comfortable.

HELMETS

When it comes to helmets, the decision to wear one can be a matter of life or death in the event of a bad spill. So obviously a helmet is the single most important piece of riding gear an OHV enthusiast can wear.

Those of us who always wear helmets often wonder what the problem is with folks who refuse to do so. Modern helmets are actually very comfortable and lightweight, providing the rider with a lot of confidence and protection from the elements. Many off-road helmets are also vented, so getting too hot is no longer a valid excuse for not wearing one. Of course, if you happen to be riding in an area where it's against the law to ride without a helmet, well you aren't going to have a choice!

There's an old saying in the off-road world: "If you've got a $10 head, buy a $10 helmet." Basically, it's warning riders to steer clear of the really cheap helmets. Not all helmets are as effective as the next, and the quality helmet makers have gone to great lengths to give their customers the best protection available.

In fact, one of the first things to look for when buying a helmet is to see if it meets one

This why ATV racers always wear a full set of safety gear whenever they're on the track. This rider not only got back up and walked away, but he was racing again later in the day! Trail riders don't necessarily have to wear a complete set of racing gear every time they ride, but the basics of a helmet, goggles, and over-the-ankle boots are a must.

TIP

A COOL WET T-SHIRT

If the riding temperatures shoot into the high 80s and 90s, you may want to soak an old T-shirt or rag with water and wrap it around your neck. As the water evaporates, it does an incredible job of cooling you down. Then, whenever you hit a water crossing, stop, dip it in the stream, and you're ready for another round of natural cooling! Soaking the jersey you're wearing works too, but it will get pretty dirty from the dust in the air.

RIDING WITH GLASSES
AND CONTACTS

For most of my riding days, I have had to wear contacts or glasses, so I have a lot of experience dealing with eyewear. I prefer wearing my soft contacts, but I always make sure that I carry a little bottle of saline solution or eye drops in case I get some small particles in my eyes during the ride. Sometimes I put a few drops in during a rest stop just to relieve the dry, dusty feeling.

As far as glasses go, most goggles will fit over glasses and some are designed specifically for that. Some helmets work better than others with glasses, so bring along your specs when buying a helmet. I found that the lighter and smaller-framed glasses worked best. I tried the prescription goggles but never felt real comfortable with them, but other riders I know felt they worked just fine.

of the two performance ratings (these are stitched on the inside of the shell and on the box). The first is the Department of Transportation (DOT) rating that shows the helmet meets a certain set of standards as a legal helmet for street and off-road use. The Snell rating (named for a sports car racer who died of head injuries in the late 1950s) signifies that the helmet goes beyond the DOT standards and can withstand even harder blows.

Most automobile, ATV, and motorcycle racers demand nothing less than a Snell rating for their headgear. Of course, the higher-quality Snell helmets are going to cost more, but you should still find plenty of choices that are reasonably priced.

Now let's face it, as with most anything that we wear, looks are an important part of the buying process. Fortunately, the style and color choices from the various manufacturers are immense. Start your new helmet search by choosing several helmet styles and colors in your price range and then begin to compare features.

Another important helmet decision is whether you want a full-face or open-face helmet. Before full-face helmets came onto the market in the early 1970s, dirt bike riders fashioned plastic mouth guards that strapped onto the bottom of the helmet. The full-face helmet eliminated the need for mouth guards and virtually all racers embraced the full-face

ATV riders have lots of choices when it comes to riding gear. Most of it is designed for both dirt bike and quad riders and some package deals in the magazines offer boots, gloves, jersey, and pants starting as low as $150. You can add a DOT-approved helmet to the package for another $50.

concept by the start of the 1980s. Off-highway vehicle riders today buy considerably more full-face helmets than open-face (full-face helmets are not necessarily more expensive). And common sense says why *not* have the extra protections of a full-face helmet (your chin and teeth are pretty vulnerable in an open-face helmet). Full-face helmets combined with goggles also offer much better protection against the elements than open-face helmets do.

The type of ATV riders who may choose an open face are typically those who utilize their quads for work or other outdoor recreations, such as hunting, fishing, ranching, or construction. Being able to

have easy access to their face while wearing their helmet and having the added visibility is a plus. Also, the chance of having a tough spill is simply not as great as that for a trail rider or racer.

There are also other features you should be aware of while checking out helmets. First off, check for air vents that can be opened or closed for hot or cold weather. Then compare the weights (a lighter helmet is much more comfortable during a long day of riding). You should also check the construction of the visor for durability.

You may also want a visor that is adjustable to your taste. Many folks who

This is one of the reasons why we wear so much protective gear. The best part is all of it is washable and is designed for easy cleaning.

ALERT!

KONK YOUR HEAD, TOSS YOUR HELMET

Nearly every helmet manufacturer recommends that you retire your helmet after a spill in which your helmet hits the ground or other obstacle. Even if you don't see any exterior damage, the helmet's crushable liner may be compromised. A hard hit from dropping it on pavement or rocks may damage the interior structure as well. This is one reason why you may want to avoid ever buying a used helmet since you don't know what kind of hits it has taken.

If you want the latest, coolest styles and the highest-quality materials, you'll be spending more than you would for the budget-priced gear. The racing crowd—which typically demands the ultimate in protection, style, fit, and durability—usually purchases top-of-the-line safety gear.

The perfect fit for a helmet is as snug as you can get it while still being comfortable.

TIP

COLOR MATTERS

If your style is all black, you may want to reconsider. Black helmets and black jerseys can make you miserable in the summer. White boots aren't such a good idea, though—you'll never get them clean!

don't ride assume that a visor on an ATV helmet is used to keep the sun out of your eyes like a baseball cap, but the primary purpose of a visor is so a rider can duck and protect his face from the dirt roost being thrown by the rider in front of him!

Getting a helmet that fits right is important for two reasons: *1)* a proper fit is much more effective in a mishap, and *2)* you won't mind wearing it all the time because it's comfortable! The best way to check fit is of course to simply try a lot of helmets on. Also be aware that a medium size in one brand may be more similar to a small in another. Some of the higher-end helmets are sold in more precise sizes such as $7^1/4$ or 8.

The perfect fit for a helmet is as snug as you can get it while still being comfortable. You should not be able to easily insert a finger between your forehead and the helmet lining. Similarly, the padding of a full-face helmet should press lightly against your cheeks, but

here you are much more likely to insert a finger or two. With the helmet in place, try to rotate it without turning your head. If the helmet turns significantly on your head (especially if it turns enough to interfere with your vision), it is too loose and you should try the next size down. If the next size down is too tight, consider trying another brand, as each helmet manufacturer has fairly unique shell shapes. Without tightening the chinstraps, shake your head briskly from left to right a few times. The helmet should follow your head and not come out of place. The same goes if you move your head up and down quickly.

Now try the retention strap system. You should be able to easily strap on the helmet you choose. Once the strap is snug, grab the helmet with both hands and move it around vigorously. Your head should be moving with the helmet.

If you're going to be wearing glasses with your helmet, make sure you try them on at this

The single most important piece of riding gear is the helmet. Make sure yours is the right fit and comfortable enough for a full day of riding. Fortunately, most of today's helmets are very lightweight and feature cooling air inlets for summer riding.

time as well. You may need a slightly looser fit in the side of your temples.

GOGGLES

The basic design of most off-road goggles is pretty much the same—flexible plastic frames and a foam perimeter that works as an air filter to keep dust and sand out, but allows for circulation to keep fogging down. More expensive goggles might feature things like no-fog coatings, light-sensitive lenses, sweat-wicking face foam, or micro-filtering vent foam.

The lenses are made from plastic rather than glass and are easily replaceable on any quality goggle. This not only allows users to replace badly scratched lenses (which scratch quite easily, especially while riding in muddy conditions), but it also lets them switch to different tinted lenses for different weather conditions.

Right behind helmets, goggles are probably the one piece of riding gear you can't do without. Dust, sand, rocks, and all sorts of debris will try to make their way into unprotected eyes while riding, and no one needs to tell you how painful and dangerous that can be!

Goggles take more of a beating during a ride than you would imagine, and the inexpensive ones (under $15) tend to not last very long. So before you buy, take a good look at the construction of the frame and especially the foam that contacts your face. Does the

foam look durable and is it glued on securely?

If you can, try the goggles on, preferably with your helmet. Make sure the goggles fit your face and that there are no gaps where sand and dust can get in. You also want to check that the frame isn't pushing on the bridge of your nose. Goggles should fit to the point where you hardly even know they're on.

Another thing to consider is that you should get goggle straps that are adjustable. In fact, look for some silicone strips on the inside of the strap to keep them from slipping down your helmet.

GOGGLE ROLL-OFFS

Roll-Offs consist of a thin, clear plastic film that is held tight against the outside of the goggle by two small drums on either end of the goggle. They are useful when a rider gets splashed with mud, as they allow a rider to simply reach up and pull on a little cord that swipes a new layer of clean plastic across the goggles.

RIDING BOOTS

Sure, many riders could probably get away with wearing work boots during their trail rides, but they'd be a lot more comfortable and much better protected with riding boots. ATV riders actually move their feet and legs quite a bit while riding, so strong and sturdy riding boots will add considerably to your riding pleasure and are well worth the price.

You don't have to tell anyone who has ever gone barehanded on a full-day of ATV riding how important riding gloves are. They'll know from the blisters and skinned knuckles that they should have had some hand protection.

TIP

I CAN'T SEE THROUGH THE FOG!

Some riders in certain weather conditions have trouble with their goggles fogging up on the inside surface. To prevent this, you can use an anti-fogging spray, made for glasses, goggles, and scuba diving masks. Any of these will work fine on the surface of your goggles to eliminate the problem.

There are basically two kinds of OHV boots on the market: motocross boots and ATV boots. They look quite similar, since the main difference is in the soles. The motocross boots don't have much of a tread on them since the riders stick their legs out and drag their feet in the corners. Of course, ATV riders don't do that and need good cleats on the bottom of their boots for walking around in the typically slippery and muddy conditions they may find themselves in during a ride. So before you begin looking at any specific boots, make sure they are ATV-specific boots.

Off-road riding boots are generally made from a combination of leather and plastic pieces with Velcro and plastic or metal buckles. Some also feature laces with a quick, one-pull tightening system.

Like the helmets, the best way to choose your boots is to first try them on. You're, of course, looking for the most comfortable fit, but be aware that new boots are very stiff at first and need to be broken in. However, you can get a good feel for them by trying them on and walking around a bit. You generally want the fit to be just a little looser than you would for other footwear. Riding boots that are too tight could get quite uncomfortable by the end of the day.

Pay special attention to the buckling system. If it seems like that particular system will be a hassle for you every time you go riding, try another. And keep in mind that it

gets considerably easier to buckle up after the initial adjustments on the straps are made for your feet and ankles.

If you're used to wearing comfortable shoes, or just want to make your boots cushier, you can add insoles just like you would with other shoes. You'll also want to get a pair of cushy, long motocross socks to go with your boot as well. Street socks really don't cut it in the off-road world.

One of the first things that typically fail on off-road boots are the buckles, so take a good look at them and make sure they fasten easily and securely. If you have a quad with a foot shifter, check to see that the left boot has a plastic toe patch. A lot of boots are also reinforced around the inside ankle/calf area, where the boots tend to rub on your machine a lot. Some boots offer a faux-suede material in that area, which helps eliminate scratches on your machine.

RIDING GLOVES

Just about every sport has its own set of gloves that are used for protection and performance. ATV riding is no exception. A sport-type glove for ATV riders is usually lightweight, vented, tight-fitting, and features padding in the palm area and protective, soft plastic pads sewn on the back of the hand and fingers.

Riding gloves keep you from getting blisters and protect your hands from debris and in the case of a spill. As an added bonus, if you stop to do some chores or have to work on your ATV, you'll be glad you already have some gloves on.

If most of your riding is done in warm weather, consider getting gloves with lots of venting and that are brightly colored, rather than black. Be sure to check out the stitching and workmanship for durability. A padded palm is a nice feature that keeps the glove from bunching upon the grip. Another sign of a good pair of gloves is if the fingers are constructed of multiple sections (which makes for a better fit when gripping the bars).

Some off-road gloves are waterproof. In summer weather, it really doesn't matter if your hands get wet, but in the spring and fall, wet, cold hands can be a real nuisance. Simply keep a pair of waterproof gloves packed in your ATV in the event of bad weather.

Winter ATV riders should consider buying snowmobile gloves. Look for plenty of insulation and a waterproof shell in these. A

Riding boots offer a ton of protection for your vulnerable ankle/foot area. Try to choose boots that have a cleated sole rather than a smooth sole that is designed for motorcycle racers. Pay special attention to the buckle system, as that is usually the first thing to give out on riding boots.

One of the first things that typically fail on off-road boots are the buckles, so take a good look at them and make sure they fasten easily and securely.

medium-weight insulated glove could also serve well in the spring and fall. Most snowmobile-type gloves are gauntlet-style, meaning they fit over the sleeves, further blocking the flow of cold air. However, be careful that you don't purchase gloves that are so bulky that it becomes difficult to use the ATVs controls.

When trying on a pair of gloves, the tips of the fingers should just touch when you interlock your hands and push down at the base of your fingers. This is a good way to tell if the gloves are the proper size. Another test is to put on a glove and make a fist as tight as you can. If the glove feels really tight over the knuckles, it may be too small. Or if the tips of your fingers feel tight, the glove may also be

too small for your hand. Try on a few different sizes and perform these tests.

RIDING PANTS

There are a lot of benefits to wearing a pair of riding pants rather than an old pair of jeans. Like most of the riding gear described here, it's all about comfort and safety. Riding pants are built with extra roominess that a day in the saddle of an ATV requires. They're also tough, easily washable, and feature pads and protection where you need it most. Besides that, they look cool.

Buying quality riding pants is like buying any other garment: look for durable material, heavy-duty stitching, etc. Buy the same waist size that you would wear in

---

TIP

OIL YOUR GOGGLES FOR DUSTY RIDING

Goggles need to breathe, which is why they have a rim of foam "air filter" around the frame. However, the foam does let a certain amount of fine dust in. If you know you're going to be riding in extremely dusty conditions, take a small amount of motor oil and apply it with the tip of a rag to the exterior of the goggle foam. It will help catch dust throughout the day. Simply clean with soap and water to get all the gunk out when you get home.

With the proper care, you can make a pair of goggles last several seasons. Most have the capability of utilizing replacement lenses if they happen to get scratched.

What a lot of riders do if they know they'll be riding in rainy, cool conditions is wear cheap plastic raingear over their riding pants.

TIP

BOOT BREAK IN

Walking around in a new pair of riding boots feels like you're wearing stiff, plastic ski boots. Your first couple of rides could be quite uncomfortable in a new pair of boots. You can avoid that by breaking in your boots ahead of time with the soaking method. Simply soak them down by filling them up with a garden hose. Then put the boots on and do some simple yard work or other chores for a couple of hours. The boots will break in much faster with this method than if you just went riding.

Dry them by hanging them upside down on a pole or a stick. Always store boots upside down or on their sides. Storing them right side up will weaken the bend where the ankle meets the top of the foot and your boots will always flop forward.

regular pants. Don't worry about the length, since riding pants are designed to be tucked into your boots. Look for pants that have reinforcements in the knee area, which is where most pants wear out first.

Some riding pants come with removable hip pads and knee pads, while others have some padding sewn in. Still others have no kneepads at all, but they can be bought separately. Knee pads are great to have if you happen to fall off your quad, but they also come in real handy if you catch something along the trail with your front wheels and come to a quick stop, slamming your knees against the front fenders or handlebars.

Most riding pants repel water for a while,

DRESS SAFELY.

Always wear your helmet, goggles, a long-sleeved shirt, gloves, long pants, and boots. At the end of the day you'll be glad you did!

but they'll eventually get wet. What a lot of riders do if they know they'll be riding in rainy, cool conditions is wear cheap plastic raingear over their riding pants. You should also buy your pants with enough room so that you can wear long underwear underneath when it starts getting cold out. Of course, hard-core winter riders will want to look for some pants from the snowmobile or skiing world. Some riding pants are specifically built for hot weather, featuring lots of ventilation.

JERSEYS

Picking out a jersey is pretty straightforward. Most of the jerseys from the major manufacturers are made from a polyester blend and are very durable. Sometimes you can still find riding jerseys made from cotton, but these tend to stain easier in muddy conditions. Like the pants, some jerseys are made with maximum venting for use in hot weather.

When buying a jersey, check its construction around the cuff and neck areas and also examine if it has any padding in the elbow or forearm area.

RIDING JACKETS

Riding jackets, also known as enduro jackets, offer lots of protection from the weather and debris. Most are incredibly durable and clean up easily in the washing machine. Some are quite water-resistant and will keep you dry in a downpour.

Enduro jackets have a lot of features you might be interested in, and it basically comes down to how much you want to spend. One of the most important things to consider, though, is the jacket's air vents in the upper arm and back area. These can be opened or closed with a zipper so you can stay warm on a cold day and cool on a hot one.

For extra cool-weather protection, look for long, snug cuffs and a pull-up collar area. Some of the nicer jackets feature soft fabric for extra comfort in those areas.

Pockets are also important. They should be deep and have a strong closure on them—you don't want stuff flying out during your ride. A small zip-up pocket on the inside of your jacket provides a good, secure place to keep your money and car keys.

RIDING GEAR CARE
YOUR GEAR WILL LAST A LONG TIME WITH A LITTLE EFFORT

Like the ATVs themselves, most riding gear is made to last. Nearly all of it is washable and will stay looking sharp even after mud rides if you take care of it well.

HELMETS

With helmets, most feature removable liners that can be thrown into the washing machine. But to stay on the safe side, don't throw this liner into the dryer; instead let it air dry. If the liner isn't removable, clean it with soap and water. Keep in mind, though, that you shouldn't use any solvents on any helmet materials—the Styrofoam inner liner can easily melt, ruining the most important part of the helmet.

If you know you are going to be riding in muddy conditions, you can make the chore of cleaning the outer shell much easier by applying ahead of time a thin coat of WD-40 or Armor-All.

GOGGLES

The most fragile part of your goggles is the lens, which scratches fairly easily. Even though it's replaceable, you can still get a lot more life out of your goggle lens by always cleaning it carefully with a soft damp cloth. If there's lots of mud dried on it, immerse the goggles in water and let them soak to get the big stuff off without scratching.

Be careful with various cleaners. Some will eat the plastic lens right up! So stick to using good old-fashioned soap and water. Also, don't store your goggles stretched on your helmet—

that will make the strap flimsy. The best place to keep them from getting scratched is to stuff them inside your helmet.

BOOTS

Following a muddy ride, you should always give your boots a good scrubbing with a brush and soap. The leather parts of your boots will also appreciate a treatment with leather oils now and then to replace the natural oils that water removes. Otherwise, your boots can get dry and cracked (deep cracking will weaken the material and eventually lead to splits).

Also try to keep the buckles free from mud and small rocks that could bend and wear the mechanisms prematurely.

GLOVES, JERSEYS, PANTS, AND RIDING JACKETS

Keeping gloves, jerseys, pants, and riding jackets clean and in good shape is not rocket science. Unless your gloves are made of real leather (few racing gloves are), they can be thrown in the washing machine with the rest of the gear listed above. For real muddy clothes, you may want to squirt them off with a hose ahead of time to get a better clean (and not gum up your washing machine).

Different materials require different washing instructions (read the label), but your best bet is to wash in cold water and then air dry your riding gear simply to avoid any damage to the plastic pieces or shrinkage.

Some jackets can be folded up into themselves and made into their own fanny pack, complete with the belts built right in.

A belt or other tightening device around the waist keeps your jacket from billowing up during your ride. Always buy your jacket a little large so you'll have room to layer with a nice heavy sweatshirt for cold-weather riding.

BASIC RIDING TECHNIQUES
GETTING PREPARED TO HIT THE TRAILS

HERE WE WILL COVER

- Pre-ride inspections
- Setting up a practice area
- Starting, shifting, and stopping
- Cornering
- Off-cambers and hills
- How to handle obstacles
- Riding strategies
- Taking an ASI RiderCourse

Before your first ride, you should take a basic safety course. One thing you'll learn is that if you can't make it up the hill and can't safely turn around, you should always keep your weight to the uphill side of the quad. Use this same technique when traveling on sidehill trails.

Of course, the best thing for every new rider to do is enroll in an ATV Safety Institute (ASI) ATV RiderCourse.

Every one of us at one time was a beginning ATV rider. We all had to survive the first-day jitters as we learned the basic techniques of riding an all-terrain vehicle. For most people, this experience is both fun and challenging. By the end of the day, new ATV riders feel a great sense of accomplishment and are excited about the new sport they've just discovered. However, like a young bird just out of the nest and learning to fly, the first day of riding can also be a bit risky. That's why safety is paramount while learning basic ATV riding skills.

Of course, the best thing for every new rider to do is enroll in an ATV Safety Institute (ASI) ATV RiderCourse. It's not expensive to take, and if you're buying a new quad, you will probably get a certificate to take the course for free. Certified ASI instructors conduct courses at various locations throughout the country. (For more on the ATV RiderCourse, see sidebar near the end of this chapter).

However, taking the course is not always possible for all riders. So in this chapter, I'll outline a step-by-step training procedure that

is similar to the field training section of the ATV RiderCourse.

KNOW YOUR MACHINE

The first thing to do is carefully read over your owner's manual and become familiar with the way your machine works. As you read the manual, sit on the ATV and get a good feel for where all the controls are— brakes, throttle, shifting, etc. Then figure out the proper procedure for starting. Where is the choke? How long should you let it warm up? Make sure you understand that all shifting is done with the throttle chopped and the revs down.

PRE-RIDE INSPECTION

Inspecting the mechanical condition of your ATV before each ride is important to minimize the chance of being injured or stranded. This also insures long enjoyment of your ATV. Remember, you can ride farther in one hour than you can walk in a day.

The first step in this process is to check

Hillclimbs require that you keep your weight to the front of the machine and use a steady throttle. Unless you are a very experienced rider, only tackle hills that you know you can safely top. The consequences of not making it up a steep hill can be quite severe with an ATV.

your tire pressure. If the tires on one side of your quad are not the same pressure as the corresponding tires on the other side, your handling will be affected. Over-inflated tires may get damaged and under-inflated tires can ruin the rims. You'll need a low-pressure tire gauge to get the job done.

Next check the wheel nuts, axle nuts, and grab the tires and rock them back and forth to try and detect worn-out bearings. Also test the action of the brake levers, throttle, and foot shifter. If your ATV features an adjustable throttle limiter, make sure the adjustment is appropriate for the rider.

You should always take a peak at the oil, fuel, and coolant levels, as well as looking for any leaks in the various systems. Then check the chains and sprockets (if applicable) for adequate adjustment, wear, and proper lubrication. Wiggle the handlebars back and forth, looking for any loose connections. Make sure you're carrying a tool kit and any other emergency equipment you may feel you need.

SET UP YOUR PRACTICE AREA

Choose a large (about 100x200 feet) flat, open practice area, free of obstacles and hazards, to use while you practice. The terrain should be flat for all the exercises described here except for the hill exercises. Practicing on a hard dirt surface will make it easier for you to learn the basic maneuvers.

If you are riding on private property, be sure you have permission from the owner. Do not do these exercises on public roads or paved surfaces. ATVs are designed for off-road use only.

For your markers, you'll need five objects—these can be milk cartons or plastic bottles with sand in them. Do not use glass bottles or other breakable items, though. You should also bring a tape measure to mark your distances, or at least measure your stride so you can pace off the distances (100 feet is approximately 35 to 40 paces).

PROPER POSTURE

The correct riding posture will help you to easily operate the controls and help you react more quickly when shifting your body weight. Proper straight-line riding posture includes:

The key to hitting trail obstacles is to keep your weight to the rear of the machine and then apply a short burst of throttle just as the front wheels hit. If you have a 4WD, make sure you put it in the 4x4 mode and then you can simply crawl over it.

Going downhill on ATVs can seem kind of scary at first, but it's actually quite simple. Keep your speed down by either going into a lower gear or applying both brakes, put your weight over the rear of the seat, and let the machine move around underneath you.

> ## TIP
>
> ### USING REVERSE GEAR
>
> Nearly all quads have a reverse gear. The ATV manufacturers wisely installed rev-limiters that are activated when reverse is engaged, severely limiting your reverse speed. Why is that? Well, the handling of a quad while traveling backwards is really funky and it's easy to loose control and tip over if you are going too fast.
>
> However, there are times when you could use more power in reverse and many ATVs feature a reverse rev-limit override button. For example, you might be stuck in a nasty mud hole and want to reverse out to drier ground. With the rev-limiter kicking in, you can't get out. Simply push the override button as you give the machine throttle and you'll get the horsepower to get you out of the situation. Whatever you do, don't use the override button to have a drag race in reverse with your buddy. That will probably end with one of you upside down.

• Head and eyes up, looking well ahead.
• Shoulders relaxed, elbows bent slightly out, away from your body.
• Hands on the handlebars.
• Knees in towards the gas tank.
• Feet on footrests, toes pointing straight ahead.

ATVs are rider-active, so to enhance the performance capabilities of the ATV, you must shift your body weight. This is especially true in maneuvers such as turning, negotiating hills, and crossing obstacles.

STARTING AND STOPPING

The first thing to work on is simply starting and stopping in a straight line. Set up two markers, B1 and B2, about 100 feet from your starting point **(see Figure 3.1)**. In first or low gear, ride to the markers (riders with a clutch will have a chance here to learn how to release it slowly) and slow down before you reach the markers. Come to a smooth, non-skidding stop using both the front and rear brakes, with your front tires between the markers.

Then, if you have a shifting model, do the course again, taking off in first and shifting to second, and then downshifting to first as you start braking. Whether you have an automatic transmission or a manual transmission ATV, do this procedure several times, increasing your speed slightly each time.

Next try a similar stopping exercise in a corner **(see Figure 3.2)**. Take turns stopping at marker C and D, increasing your speed as you feel more comfortable. Be careful to not overshoot the corner or skid while braking.

Figure 3.1

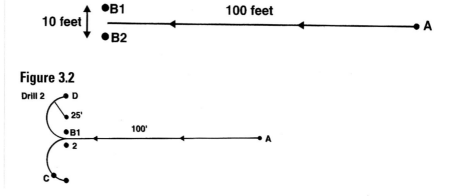

Figure 3.2

TURNING BASICS

The following basic turning techniques apply to ATVs being ridden at low to moderate speeds:

- Move your body weight forward and to the inside of the turn.
- Turn the handlebars while looking in the direction of the turn.
- As you increase your speed or turn more sharply, move your body weight farther toward the inside of the turn to maintain your balance.
- If your ATV starts to tip while turning, lean your body farther into the turn while gradually reducing the throttle and making the turn wider, if possible.

There are three drills you can use in the field to practice turning. Start with a large oval made with two markers **(see Figure 3.3)**. Ride around the outside, making left turns and then try some to the right. Do not shift gears during the exercise. The next drill is practicing tight circles **(see Figure 3.4)**. You can use the same markers in the same position for this exercise as well as the next one. Simply ride around the markers and decrease the radius of the turns so that you are making tighter turns and then ride around marker B to the right.

The final turning drill **(see Figure 3.5)** is a figure eight exercise. As your skills increase, move the marker closer together (25 feet apart) so that the figure eight becomes smaller. During these exercises, be careful to not tip or make wide turns. To compensate, slow down, lean your body into the turn, put more weight up front, use more effort to turn the handlebars, and look in the direction of the turn.

GOING UP HILLS

Climbing hills improperly could cause loss of control or cause the ATV to overturn. So it's a good idea to remember these tips:

- Some hills are too steep for your abilities. Use your common sense. If the hill you are approaching looks too steep, it probably is.
- Some hills are just too steep for your ATV, regardless of your abilities.
- Never ride past the limit of your visibility; if you cannot see what is on or over the crest of a hill, slow down until you have a clear view.
- The key to being a good hill rider is to keep your weight uphill at all times.

When approaching an uphill climb, you should:

- Shift the ATV into a lower gear and speed up *before* climbing the hill so you

The best way to learn how to ride an ATV is to take an ATV Safety Institute (ASI) ATV RiderCourse. In the one-day session, an accredited instructor will get you started on the right foot in this great sport.

Figure 3.3

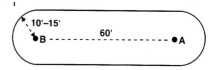

Figure 3.4

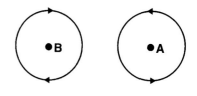

Figure 3.5

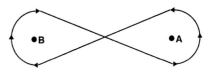

Many dealers and ATV manufacturers offer free ASI training with the purchase of a new ATV. The fees for extra family members are quite reasonable as well.

During the ATV RiderCourse, students go through a series of field trials as they learn the basics of starting, stopping, turning, climbing hills, and overcoming obstacles. This chapter details many of those procedures for those riders who can't make it to an ASI course.

Figure 3.6

Figure 3.7

Figure 3.8

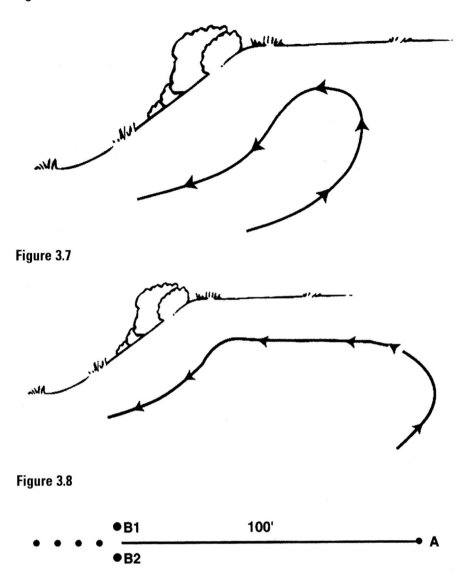

can maintain momentum.

- When approaching the uphill climb, move up on the seat and lean forward, or stand and position your torso over the front wheels.

As you are climbing, you may need to shift to a lower gear to prevent lugging or stalling the engine. To shift into a lower gear on a hill, remember these points:

- Keep your body weight forward as you prepare to shift gears. For steeper hills, lean forward as much as possible.
- Shift quickly while momentarily releasing the throttle; this will help keep the front wheels from lifting.

If you do not have enough power to reach the top of the hill, but still have forward momentum and enough room to turn around safely, keep these in mind:

- Keep your weight uphill.
- Make a U-turn before you lose speed.
- Proceed downhill in lower gear, keeping your weight to the uphill side.

If you are riding uphill and lose all forward momentum:

- Keep your weight uphill and apply both the front and rear brakes to come to a stop. *Never* allow the ATV to roll backward.
- Apply the parking brake while keeping your weight uphill.
- Dismount on the uphill side or to either side if pointed straight uphill.
- Hang on to the machine until your riding pals can come up and help you safely turn it around or inch it back down the hill.
- Do not attempt to ride backward down a hill. Should you begin rolling backward,

HIDDEN OBSTACLES

Many trails are just barely wide enough for ATVs to go down. In the middle of summer when the weeds are at the height of their growth, they can hide big rocks and cut logs alongside (and sometimes in the middle of) the trail. Be careful when riding in dusty conditions as well, as the dust can obscure big rocks on the trail. When it's dusty out, simply keep your distance from the rider in front to have a more pleasant, and safer, ride.

In this sport, not everyone has to be sliding around corners and jumping over logs to have fun. Many riders are simply content to cruise along and enjoy the scenery of our great outdoors on casual trail rides.

do not apply the rear brake abruptly. Only using the rear brake or applying it abruptly could cause the ATV to roll over backward.

GOING DOWN HILLS AND TRAVERSING A SLOPE

Always check the terrain carefully before you start down any hill. Choose a downhill path that is as straight as possible, with a minimum of obstacles. Shift your weight to the rear of the machine and use a low gear. On steeper downward slopes, straighten, but do not lock, your knees and elbows. Then bend forward sharply at the waist so that your posterior is over the back of the seat. Utilize both brakes to gradually slow down.

When you go across a slope rather than directly up or down, it is called traversing and requires additional attention. Avoid traversing slopes with excessively slippery, rough, or loose surfaces.

Here are some basic guidelines for traversing:
- Lean your upper body uphill.
- When riding on soft terrain, you may need to turn your front wheels gently uphill to keep your ATV on a straight line across the hill.
- If your ATV begins to tip, turn the front wheels downhill if the terrain allows. If the terrain does not permit, dismount on the uphill side immediately.
- Avoid making sudden throttle changes.

HILL DRILLS

For this exercise, select an easy hill, free of obstructions (easy to climb on foot). Start your approach to the hill by accelerating before the base of the hill. Shift into a lower gear at the base of the hill if necessary to maintain momentum while climbing the hill. Turn the ATV to the left, in an arc, before you reach the top **(see Figure 3.6)**. Keep turning, using your remaining momentum until you are facing downhill. During the turn, you'll have to shift your weight to the uphill side of the quad.

Descend the hill in a lower gear, and as you descend, slow down by applying the brakes. When going downhill, keep your weight to the rear of the machine. Then practice with your weight to the right. The key to successfully performing this exercise is to shift your weight smoothly from forward (as you climb) to the uphill side (as you turn) and the rear (as you descend). For smooth weight shifts, rise up slightly off the seat.

To practice traversing **(see Figure 3.7)**, select an easy hill free of obstructions. Start your approach and accelerate before the base of the hill. Turn the ATV to the left, ride across the slope, and then ride down the hill. Repeat the exercise to the right.

QUICKER STOPS AND QUICKER TURNS

To practice quicker stops, set up the markers as indicated in **Figure 3.8**. Start at marker A and ride

toward B1-B2 in second gear. Be sure to maintain your speed until you pass B1-B2. When the ATV passes markers B1-B2, stop as quickly and safely as you can. Notice where you stop. Put some sort of marker down there. Do it again and stop smoothly and quickly, but in a shorter distance. Make your first two attempts in second gear and then shift to higher gears. Keep your head and eyes up with your weight towards the back of the ATV while performing quick braking.

Being able to make quick turns can come in real handy when you need to avoid obstacles on the trail. Practice this by putting five markers down at 35-foot intervals. Travel to the left of the first marker and then to the right of the second and continue until you reach the last marker. At first, practice at slow speeds, and then gradually increase your speed. After you have mastered this, move the markers closer together. Do not move them closer than 18 feet apart.

The key to doing the quick turn exercise is to shift your weight quickly to initiate the turn. To shift your weight effectively, rise up slightly standing on the footrests, quickly move your hips, and lean your body to the inside of each turn. To go left, apply a slight left turn to the front wheels, quickly lean left, and apply a short burst of throttle. To go right, do the opposite. Do not look at the next marker you are approaching. Look ahead and do not fixate on a marker.

HOW TO HANDLE OBSTACLES

It's inevitable that you'll have to go over some obstacles out on the trails. Whether it's a rut, boulder, log or ridge, there's a way to get over it smoothly and safely. Here's a step-by-step method of handling obstacles:

- Stand up on the seat as you approach the obstacle with your arms and knees bent.
- Keep a firm grip on the handlebars to keep the ATV pointed straight ahead.
- Apply a small amount of throttle as the front wheels meet the obstacle. Release the throttle as soon as the front wheels have gone over the obstacle.
- Lean forward slightly once the front wheels have gone over the obstacle in order to remove weight from the rear wheels. The throttle must be released before the rear wheels hit.•
- Choose a small obstacle for your initial practice. A small rut, mound, or small log will work fine. Approach the obstacle at

walking speed and as close to a 90-degree angle as possible.

TRAIL RIDING STRATEGIES

To get the most out of your ride, you have to know the land you are riding on and what your machine can do. Carefully choose the places you ride. You should always use existing trails. Stay away from terrain where you do not belong, such as dangerous slopes and impassable swamps. Watch carefully for sharp bumps, holes, ruts or obstacles.

An expert rider stays out of trouble by handling the ATV well and avoiding any risky situation. Learn to read the trail as you ride. An expert rider looks well ahead on the trail. Know what is coming up and be prepared to react long before you get there. Be constantly alert for hazards.

Go at a speed that is proper for the terrain, visibility, operating conditions, and your experience. By scanning far enough down the trail, you will be able to pick the best "lines" (or safest paths of travel) around or over hazards or small obstacles. As you approach a hazard, do not fixate on it. Instead, continue to search for other clues in the environment and adjust your speed well in advance.

An expert rider stays out of trouble by handling the ATV well and avoiding any risky situation.

Chapter 4

KIDS AND ATVs
GETTING THEM STARTED RIGHT

The sport of ATV riding and racing is something the whole family can participate in. Most manufacturers offer a model for just about every size and skill level.

Because parents know their kids best, you are in the best position to decide when your son or daughter is ready to ride.

Off-road riding is a great family activity. It's a chance for young people to learn new skills and develop self-confidence, and parents find exploring the out-of-doors a wonderful way to spend time with their kids.

Along with the fun and adventure, off-roading involves special responsibilities for parents and young people. Even the smallest ATV is relatively heavy and should be respected and never treated like a toy.

So is your youngster even ready to ride? Because parents know their kids best, you are in the best position to decide when your son or daughter is ready to ride. Riding readiness can vary widely from one person to another, and there's no sure way to determine whether a given boy or girl is ready. However, the following guidelines can help you reach a decision.

ARE THEY BIG ENOUGH?

To safely ride off-road, a person must be large enough and strong enough to easily reach and operate the controls. To see how a young rider measures up, first have him or her sit on the vehicle you are considering. Are their arms long enough to turn the handlebars all the way to the right and to the left? Are their hands big enough and strong enough to work the brake levers, the throttle, and other hand controls? Can their feet comfortably reach and operate the brake and other foot controls?

Next have the young person stand up on the footrests while he or she holds onto the handgrips. See if there is at least three inches between the vehicle seat and the youngster's seat of the pants. A rider needs at least three inches of clearance so they can rise off the seat for comfort, balance, and visibility.

COORDINATION AND JUDGMENT

Off-road riders need good hand-eye coordination, agility, and a sense of balance. If your son or daughter is good at riding a bicycle, skateboarding, playing baseball, or soccer, he or she will probably do fine on an ATV.

Because riders need to think quickly and react appropriately, it's important to ask yourself if your youngster analyzes problems and comes to logical conclusions. Do they understand the relationship between unsafe actions and consequences? Do they follow instructions? Do they understand that people have different abilities and accept their own limits?

Try to be honest as you evaluate riding readiness. If a young person is too small, has poor coordination, takes unnecessary risks, or doesn't make good judgments, they need more time to mature before riding off-road.

WHAT SHOULD KIDS WEAR?

Before a youngster rides off-road, you'll need to provide him or her with a few basic safety items, and make sure they wear them on *every* ride. The most valuable piece of safety equipment is a high-quality motorcycle helmet with a label showing approval by the U.S. Department of Transportation (DOT). The helmet should also fit snugly and be securely fastened before riding.

Other important safety wear includes goggles, sturdy boots, gloves, long pants, and a long-sleeved shirt or jacket.

HOW MUCH TRAINING AND SUPERVISION WILL THEY NEED?

Providing good instruction is a key responsibility of parents. As a first step, you should read the owner's manual together with your son or daughter, and make sure he or she understands the instructions and cautions.

Next will come a period of hands-on training and practice. Whether you serve as a primary instructor or arrange for a qualified teacher, plan on attending all instruction and practice sessions. This may take some time, but no one is better able than *you* to evaluate your child's progress.

Remember, even after young people become skilled off-road riders they still need adult supervision on every ride. If you can't personally ride with your youngster, you'll need to make sure a qualified and caring adult will be there.

PICKING THE RIGHT-SIZED ATV

Here's what you'll see posted at nearly every dealership in the United States:

- ATVs with an engine size less than 70cc are recommended for youngsters 6 years or older.
- ATVs with an engine size 70–90cc are recommended for youngsters 12 years or older.
- ATVs with an engine size greater than 90cc are recommended for people at least 16 years old.

In a voluntary agreement with the government dating back to the late 1980s, the dealers, in fact, can't knowingly sell an ATV to a family that plans on disobeying the above age/engine size limitations.

However, common sense tends to muddy the waters on this particular topic. On the one hand, even though the child is of the recommended age for a particular ATV, not all youngsters have the strength, skills, or judgment needed to operate the vehicle safely. On the other hand, there are many teenagers under 16 who, due to their size and maturity, are fully capable of safely operating ATVs

Youth quads are specifically designed for certain age and size ranges. Make sure your kid can easily reach all the controls as well as being able to stand up and get their weight off the seat.

Youth ATV racing is very popular in many parts of the country. Quite a few models can be raced with just a few modifications, and the amount of maintenance and repairs are usually less than that for full-sized ATVs.

One of the biggest keys to keeping your child safe while riding ATVs is to always have adult supervision.

larger than 90cc. The final decision of course is up to the parents and, as with any kind of risk sport, safety should be the number one priority when choosing the proper-sized ATV for your child.

STATE LAWS

Laws regarding children on ATVs vary considerably from state to state. Some states are not regulated at all when it comes to youngsters on ATVs, while others have quite a few rules and regulations. In most cases, the rules apply only to riders who are utilizing public lands and trails. For example, in California, operators under 18 years of age must either have an ATV safety certificate of his or her own, or be supervised by an adult with an ATV safety certificate. In addition, a parent or guardian must directly supervise children under 14 years old. California also states that the ATV should be of the appropriate size as labeled by the manufacturer.

The same rules that govern adults in California, such as always wearing a helmet, not riding double, and using a safety whip (flag) in the dunes, also apply to kids.

Before you go riding on public lands, check with your local land managers such as parks and recreation, Forest Service, Department of Natural Resources, or fish and game officials to see what laws govern you and your children while riding ATVs in your state.

When learning how to ride an ATV, choose an open, obstacle-free area to practice on. Sometimes kids on quads seem to act like magnets around trees, parked cars, and buildings.

ATV SAFETY TRAINING FOR YOUNGSTERS
THE BEST WAY TO LEARN

Like the training for adults, children are also eligible to take the ATV RiderCourse that is offered by the ATV Safety Institute (ASI). Courses regularly take place at various locations throughout the country. If you are buying a new ATV, your child may be eligible for free training; otherwise there is a modest fee.

During the course, riders will learn how to do a proper pre-ride inspection, ride in a variety of conditions, and negotiate obstacles. You'll also get the latest information on protective gear, local laws about ATV use, and finding places to ride in your area.

If you are buying a gift ATV for your child, you can complete the ATV RiderCourse on an adult-sized ATV before taking delivery of the youth model, and be better prepared to supervise your child. (Your child may take the course before or after you bring the ATV home).

The ATV RiderCourse is only conducted on ATVs of the size recommended for the rider's age. For riders younger than 16, a parent or guardian should be present at the training site. For riders younger than 12, a parent must be present during the entire course.

For the rider training location nearest you, call (800) 887-2887 or see the group's website at www.atvsafety.org.

TIP

THROTTLE LIMITERS MAKE LEARNING SAFER

Most mini ATVs feature throttle limiters that make your youngster's first rides considerably safer. The limiters are a very simple device—they're just a screw that restricts the thumb throttle and can be adjusted to virtually any speed.

As you watch your child progress with his or her riding skills, you can simply dial-in more speed. Some mini ATVs also come with a kill switch tether, which is a rope that the parent or instructor holds on to as he or she jogs alongside the rider. If there's any indication that the child is losing control, the adult simply pulls the rope and kills the engine.

RIDING RESPONSIBLY
ETHICAL RIDERS STAY SAFER AND HELP KEEP TRAILS OPEN

Chapter 5

HERE WE WILL COVER

- ATV safe-riding rules
- Treading lightly
- Sharing the trails
- Rules and regulations
- ATVs and hunting
- Riding in a group

If you ever think about jumping off the tops of sand dunes, have your buddies "spot" for you so you don't land on anyone coming up the other way. And don't forget your safety whip! It's the law at nearly every dune riding area in the country.

Responsible riders tend to be the ones who seem to never get hurt.

Basically, two of the worst-case scenarios for ATV riders are *a)* having an accident during a ride, or *b)* seeing your favorite riding areas get shut down. The first one leaves you at best with bumps and bruises on your body and machine, while the other results in your beloved quad sitting on the front lawn with a big For Sale sign on the handlebars. Both of these sorry situations appear to be out of your control. Or are they?

Riding responsibly will dramatically decrease your chances of ever getting hurt or causing your favorite riding areas to close their gates. In many ways, responsible and ethical riders also have a higher-quality ATVing experience. Knowing that you're making all the right moves out on the trail allows you to relax and have even more fun.

OK, now that you're convinced that this is the way to go, what does it really mean to be a responsible rider? Isn't it simply a matter of using common sense and common courtesy? Well, yes, a lot of it is. However, there are many potentially dangerous and destructive

behaviors that go unnoticed by novice (and even experienced!) riders. Some of these behaviors endanger us and others, the wildlife, and the environment, or just plain tick off other outdoor recreationists.

SAFETY FIRST

Responsible riders tend to be the ones who seem to never get hurt. Now responsible doesn't necessarily equate with being slow, nor does it mean that one can never have any fun by sliding sideways around corners or sailing off jumps. Quite the contrary. Many fast ATV riders also happen to be very responsible riders. They ride in control and always wear the proper safety gear (mostly because they know it really works).

They think ahead about the other OHV that may be approaching in the opposite direction, around the blind corner. They see the stump poking out of the grass at the edge of the trail and have the skill to slow down in time and miss it. They say no to drugs and alcohol, and they avoid riding on

There are certain trail riding rules one should follow when traveling with a group to keep from getting separated or stranded. One is to make sure you wait for the rider behind you when you come to an intersection!

roads with cars and trucks. They're the riders who go home at the end of the day with all the skin intact on their knees, elbows, and chins. They're the ones who get to tell all their pals on Monday what a great weekend they had!

As discussed earlier in the introduction, riding ATVs is a potentially dangerous activity. Like every other high-excitement sport, hundreds of people get injured, and sometimes even killed on ATVs every year. That's why if there is any one section of this book you should always abide by, the following is it. There's an excellent chance that if you follow the nine primary *Golden Rules of Safe ATVing*, listed in the following paragraphs, whenever you go riding, you probably will never get injured on an ATV (also see the Play it Safe Alert! in this chapter).

NINE GOLDEN RULES OF SAFE ATVING

1. Always wear the appropriate safety gear. At minimum, this should include a helmet, shatter-resistant eye protection, long pants, long-sleeved shirt, and over-the-ankle boots.

2. If you have never ridden before, take an approved training course. Call ASI toll-free (800) 887-2887.

3. Only carry passengers if your ATV is specifically designed to do so. Carrying passengers can alter the balance of the machine, causing a loss of control.

4. Ride an ATV that is the right size for you. Children riding ATVs meant for adults are recipes for disaster (see Chapter 4 for more on kids and quads).

5. Supervise riders younger than 16; ATVs are not toys, no matter the size.

Some communities allow riders to utilize parts of city streets to link up trail systems, but special care should be taken whenever you ride ATVs on paved roads.

Try to avoid riding trails when the conditions are really muddy. The quad's tires can form big ruts that add to erosion problems and make the trail hard to navigate when things dry up. Some trails are actually closed to all OHV traffic when the conditions are bad.

6. Cars and ATVs don't mix. Ride only on designated trails; avoid riding on public roads and paved surfaces.

7. Always ride at a speed that is safe for you and the terrain.

8. Never ride under the influence of alcohol or other drugs.

9. Always ride in control. Ride within your abilities and your machine's capabilities. Never attempt anything that is beyond your skill level.

TREAD LIGHTLY

The *Golden Rules of Safe ATVing* serve to protect yourself and other riders. However, when it comes to keeping trails and ride areas open, it's the environment that needs protection as well. That's when you need to "tread lightly."

There is in fact an organization called TreadLightly!—which serves to educate many outdoor recreation groups, including ATV

Many trail systems run through, or skirt around, private property. Always respect private property by staying on the trail, closing all gates behind you, and never littering!

and dirt bike riders, 4x4 drivers, mountain bikers, boaters, snowmobilers, hikers, equestrians, and hunters. Its mission is to encourage recreationists to tread lightly in the outdoors, leaving as little evidence as possible that they were ever there. The reasons for this are two-fold: to leave other outdoor recreationists and future generations with an unspoiled environment and to ensure that the great outdoors will continue to be accessible to a wide variety of users.

Fortunately, the trails themselves are not considered a detriment to the environment. Hikers make trails, deer make trails, and even the pioneers made trails (some of which are still in existence and being used today).

Rather, it's other destructive behaviors that the TreadLightly! program targets. Doing our part to keep environmental impacts to a minimum is certainly in our best interest and is not very difficult.

LEAVE NO TRACE

• Protect your riding privileges by staying on existing roads or trails. Cross-country travel on ATVs can create a network of new tracks or trails that cause soil erosion and damage to fish and wildlife habitats. Cross-country travel can also spread invasive species, which can ruin habitat. Do not contribute to resource damage and habitat destruction by creating new tracks for others to follow.

Only enter creeks and streams at the designated trail crossing and keep your speed down to avoid muddying up the water too much. Using a shallow stream as a trail may seem like fun, but it can wreak havoc with the wildlife as well as get all OHVs kicked out of the ride area.

> ### ANECDOTE
>
> ### ABUSE IT OR LOSE IT
>
> In the early 1990s, I went to a big ATV mud run held in a Louisiana swamp located on state land. No one was wearing helmets, many quads had two, even three people on board, littering along the trail was rampant, and coolers filled with beer were the number one thirst quencher. They don't have that mud run anymore. I wonder why . . .

> ### ANECDOTE
>
> ### PINNED!
>
> I have to admit that when I was younger I sometimes went riding by myself. In the years since, I have been pinned underneath a quad twice, once under water. Luckily, I was riding with a group. I don't think I would have gotten out of those situations if there wasn't someone there to help me. I now take "Never Ride Alone" quite seriously.

• User-created trails are often poorly located within riparian zones or on steep slopes creating vegetation and soil impacts. Don't make the problem worse by continuing to use these routes.

• Wheel tracks in wet meadows can be like footprints in cement—they often don't heal. Avoid the use of ATVs in wet areas or during wet conditions. Even though the lighter-weight and low-pressure tires reduce impacts, ATVs can still do serious damage to wet areas.

• You should also avoid riding over small trees and shrubs. Trampled vegetation not only looks bad, but also damages critical wildlife habitat and contributes to soil erosion.

• In addition, ride in the middle of the trail to avoid widening it. Trail widening is unsightly and expensive to repair.

• Honor seasonal and permanent trail closures.

• Never harass wildlife or domestic animals that you may encounter while riding. Always view wildlife from a respectful distance.

• Never litter. Always carry out what you carry in. Carry a trash bag with you to pack out your own and even other people's trash that you may come upon.

• Protect and respect cultural resources, such as old cabins, historic mining sites, fossil areas, and traditional cultural properties. They are an important part of our heritage; leave them for others to enjoy.

• To prevent the spread of noxious weeds, wash your ATV after you ride. Weed seeds are caught in the tires and caked-on mud.

• Keep your exhaust system quiet. Don't buy loud aftermarket pipes, and repack your stock muffler as needed.

• Cross streams only at designated crossings. Try not to splash and spin your wheels excessively. Erosion from stream banks and creek crossings can harm survival of native fish.

• When you come to a gate, leave it as you found it.

SHARING THE TRAILS

Horseback riders, mountain bikers, and hikers also enjoy many of the same public trails that allow OHV use. When serious conflicts arise between trail user groups, the losing party is typically the "motorized" recreationists, who end up losing their trail rights. How the non-motorized public views us is of utmost importance when it comes to land access issues. There are a couple ways we as OHV riders can put our best foot forward and avoid user-group conflicts. These include the following:

• Always yield the right-of-way to non-motorized trail users.

• When encountering hikers or horses on the trail, pull over and shut off your engine. With horses, remove your helmet (horses are sometimes startled by them) and let them pass out of sight before restarting.

OK, this is an example of what NOT to do when it comes to ATV riding. Now picture these guys having a few beers and then riding their quad on the highway—certainly a recipe for disaster.

TIP

DEFENSIVE RIDING

Riding ATVs requires some of the same skills and concentration that driving a car on the highway does. To avoid trouble, you have to think defensively. Is there a big rock hidden in that bush on the edge of the trail? Could another rider be coming around that blind corner up ahead? Could the quad you're riding behind suddenly swerve or stop in front of you? Have fun while you're riding, but always keep an eye open for trouble before it happens.

When overtaking others, pass in a safe and courteous manner.
• Whenever you're riding near parking or camping areas, keep your speed way down. Don't kick up dust or make a lot of noise with your engine.
• Always yield to any users (motorized included) who are traveling uphill.

PLANNING AHEAD

Responsible ATV riders generally don't get themselves into situations that involve the words "search parties" and "rescue crews."

They avoid those scenarios by following the tips listed here:
• Ride with a partner. It is really hard to ride an ATV with a broken arm! Riding solo can leave you vulnerable in case of an accident or breakdown.
• Check that your OHV is in proper working condition, all fluids are topped off, and there are no loose or broken parts.
• Contact the land manager for area restrictions, and if crossing private property, be sure to ask permission from the landowners.
• Be certain each rider in your party has a map

More and more ride areas are requiring that all OHVs meet a certain sound limit. The rangers will check your noise level with a sound meter and you can get kicked out or get a fine if you exceed the limit.

TIP

SET THE BAD APPLES STRAIGHT

Remember that other recreationists judge all ATV riders by the conduct of any rider encountered. If you observe another rider violating rules or laws, ask them to comply. If they don't, report them to the appropriate authorities so that you protect your right to ride.

Invasive weed species are an environmental concern in many parts of the country. Do your part by thoroughly washing your quad after every ride to get all the dirt and seeds off before traveling to another ride area. Some ride areas like this one in Minnesota offer a free washing bay.

TIP

NOISY OHVs ARE PUBLIC ENEMY NO.1

A recent poll of land-access advocates found that the sound issue is the number one problem facing ATV and dirt bike riders in this country. Established riding areas are closing because of noise complaints from neighbors; new ride parks are being squelched for the same reasons.

With the advent of high-performance four-strokes and the popularity of add-on racing exhausts, the problem is at an all-time high. The best thing a trail rider can do is to keep his or her exhaust stock (for more on aftermarket exhausts, see Chapter 6).

BE KIND TO BIG AND LITTLE CRITTERS.

Chasing animals is wrong!

and knows where the group is headed. If you become separated, stay on the correct trail and let the group find you. Taking different trails could result in you becoming lost.

• Know your machine's fuel range and plan accordingly.

• Check the weather forecast before leaving home. For winter riders in mountainous areas, always check the avalanche forecast.

• Always tell someone where you are going and when you will return. Provide them with a map of your intended riding area.

• Bring along a proven lifesaver—your cell phone!

• Be prepared for any emergency. Always carry a tool kit and spare parts, a tire repair kit, tow strap, a first aid kit, and survival equipment when you ride. Carry plenty of extra food, water, and fuel.

KNOW THE RIDE AREA'S RULES AND REGULATIONS

Before you think about going to any public riding area, know all the rules and regulations. This will not only keep you from being sent home as soon as you arrive, but it could keep you from getting a ticket (or even worse, from getting hurt). There are several ways to find out what the rules and regulations are: the Internet

DEFINITION

Spark Arrestor: All stock ATVs come with a U.S. Forest Service–approved spark arrestor inside the muffler. The point of a spark arrestor is to simply keep hot pieces of carbon buildup (sparks) from flying out the exhaust and starting a grass or forest fire. Many ride areas, especially in the dry western states, require working spark arrestors on all OHVs and the rangers will sometimes check for them. Some aftermarket racing exhausts don't have spark arrestors and, unless a rider adds one on, would be illegal at some riding areas.

TIP

DON'T GET SENT HOME!

Picture this: You've just traveled four hours to a really neat ride area. When you enter the gate, the ranger checks to make sure everything is legal. Oops! You don't have (pick any one of the following): a helmet, the proper registration sticker, or a safety whip, an exhaust that passes the sound test, a spark arrestor, safety certificate for the kids, etc. Ya know what? You're going to get sent home. Or at the very least, waste half the day trying to remedy the situation. The solution is simple: Find out ahead of time what the ride area requires before you pack up the trailer.

KNOW YOUR RIDING LIMITS
GOING BEYOND THEM WILL HURT!

After your first couple of days of riding, you should have a pretty good feel about what your skill level is. Hopefully, you were taking it real easy on those first rides and didn't already try to tackle anything that was over your head.

OVERCONFIDENCE = TROUBLE

ATVs tend to be kind of deceiving since, unlike a dirt bike or bicycle, quads stand up on their own. It makes them seem like anyone can ride them anywhere, on any terrain. In many ways this is true and that is much of the appeal of riding ATVs. However, some riders, usually beginning riders, get overconfident and don't realize what happens when a quad hits a bump, rock, or log at speed . . . or they think that steep hillclimbs can be tackled by simply pushing the thumb throttle.

The key is to take all things slowly at first. If you want to learn how to go off jumps, try little ones first. If you want to slide around corners, let your rear tires slip just a little until you feel comfortable getting more sideways. Riders who try right off the bat to ride like their more experienced buddies are sure to get in trouble before the end of the day.

PACE IT

Never let other riders in your group push you to go faster than what you're comfortable with. That's a common mistake that can result in you sailing off the trail into the trees or rocks.

Sometimes riders are put in positions of tackling terrain that is beyond their capabilities. If you see a section that appears to be too tough for your skill level, don't be afraid to set the parking brake and let one of the other more experienced riders take your machine through. It might be a bit humbling, but it's definitely the smart thing to do.

ALWAYS STAY ON THE TRAIL.
Riding off-trail damages the land and is dangerous!

Some ATV trails are what land managers call multiple-use. In other words, you may encounter hikers, horseback riders, and mountain bikers while you're exploring the trails. Treat them in a safe and courteous manner and you'll have a greater chance of seeing that trail stay multiple-use. Keep in mind that motorized users are usually the first to go in trail access conflicts.

(search for the name of the ride area), by phone, or by picking up a brochure on the ride area.

Begin your search by determining which land management agency runs the show. Privately held ride areas and parks are becoming more and more common and adhere to their own set of rules, which can be quite different from the ride areas run by government agencies.

Because the rules and regulations at riding areas throughout the country differ considerably, there are a wide variety of rules. However, below is an example of some of the regulations you will encounter.

TYPICAL RULES AND REGULATIONS

• Wear your helmet. Some areas require all riders to wear a helmet while others do not. Some require them only for children under a certain age. But I recommend that everyone always wears a helmet when trail riding.

• Have a registration sticker, decal, or plate. Many states with public ride areas require a sticker. Most will honor out-of-state stickers, but some do not.

• Carry safety whips or flags. These are generally required at all dune ride areas and attach to the rear grab bar. They cost around $10 to $20 and are sometimes sold near the ride area.

• Be aware of seasonal closures. Many ride areas prohibit ATV use during wet or snowy times of the year. Some even close down during the summer if conditions get bad, so be sure to call ahead of time.

• Use spark arrestors. This is more of a concern in the western states. At some parks, the rangers check for a spark arrestor on every OHV coming through the gate.

• Stay on the trail at all times. Most state and national forests strictly enforce this rule. Other parks, such as those at sand dunes, allow free ride, cross-country travel. Some ride areas have special free ride areas set aside (mud bogs, small dunes, dried lakes, etc.)

• Know the rules about riding double. Some areas allow it, others do not (see the What About Two-Up ATVs? Alert! in this chapter).

• Know the speed limit. Some sections of a ride area may have certain speed limits

Rangers do a stationary sound check on your ATV to make sure it meets the decibel limit for that particular ride area. Currently, all riders on state lands in California must meet a 96 dBa limit.

(along the beach, near the parking or camping areas, etc.). Some multiple-use trails may have a set speed limit for the entire trail system.

DEFINITION

Multiple-use trails: Many public OHV trails are called multiple-use trails. This generally means that other outdoor recreationists such as hikers, horseback riders, and mountain bikers are allowed to use the same trails as the dirt bikes and ATVs. Sometimes some of the users are prohibited for one reason or another (such as ATVs on single-track dirt bike trails). Always treat the other users with respect or it might be the ATV symbol on the sign that has the circle and slash through it next year.

TIP

BLM, DNR, SFS, & USFS

While trying to determine the various rules and regulations for your ride area you may have to contact the BLM or USFS. What the heck is that, you ask? Well, the primary public land mangers in the United States are the Bureau of Land Management (BLM) and the United States Forest Service (USFS), which oversees the National Forests. Most states have a State Forest Service (that may go by the acronym SFS) as well as a Department of Natural Resources (DNR), but that could also go under another name, depending on the state.

• Carry a safety certificate. Some states require proof that riders under a certain age have taken a safety-training course. Some have limits as to just how young a rider can be (see Chapter 4).

• Know the sound limit. This relatively new regulation is popping up at ride areas all over the country. Rangers do a stationary sound check on your ATV to make sure it meets the decibel limit for that particular ride area. Currently, all riders on state lands in California must meet a 96 dBa limit. Most stock quads easily pass the test (for more on sound limits and aftermarket exhausts, see Chapter 6).

• Check your headlight. If the ride area allows night riding, you'd better have a working headlight!

• Know the rules about washing your ATV. With all the concern over invasive weeds, some riding areas require riders to wash their machines at the provided washing station to get rid of any seeds stuck on the quads.

• Know the rules about riding on public roads. Virtually all states allow riders to safely cross from one side of the road to the other at a 90-degree angle. Some states and communities actually allow riders to legally operate their ATVs on public roads (either limited or unlimited), and some ATVs are even licensed to ride on the street (with some modifications such as turn signals, tires, etc).

A little friendly public relations with other trail users can go a long way in the general public's view of our sport.

Know the rules and regulations of your riding area and always follow them. A few bad apples will spoil it for everyone else.

TRAIL RIDING IN A GROUP
HOW TO STAY SAFE, AVOID GETTING LOST, AND HAVE FUN!

There are certain things you need to pay attention to when trail riding with a group. There's a lot more to it than simply following the guy in front of you. Before you begin, everyone should have some idea of where you're going and if possible everyone should have his or her own trail map.

Next, you decide who is going to lead and who is going to bring up the rear (also known as the "sweep"). Generally, you want the leader and the sweep to be experienced riders, preferably guys or gals who have been on the trail before. The person in the rear also has to be willing to give the slowest riders room and not to "push" them along at speeds they are not comfortable with.

YOU'RE RESPONSIBLE FOR
THE RIDER BEHIND YOU
The leader, of course, makes the decision as to which trails to follow. However, whenever he comes upon a Y or T intersection (or anything that looks like there might be a choice between trails), he must slow to make sure that the rider behind him clearly sees which way the group will be going. Then the second rider makes sure the third rider knows and so on. The most important thing to remember when riding in a group is *you are always responsible for the rider directly behind you.*

If the rider behind you never shows up, you stop and go back and look for the missing rider. Then the rider in front of, and in charge of, you, will stop and turn back, until it goes all the way up the line to the leader. At that point, the leader rides back and gathers any riders stopped along the way as they go back for the missing or downed rider. So in other words, while riding in a group, you should occasionally peek behind to see that the rider you are responsible for is still there.

LOST? STAY PUT!
If you are the rider with the problem (mechanical, physical, or you simply think

you're lost), wait for the riders behind you to catch up and the ones in front to come back. If you're lost because you are at a Y or T intersection and don't know which way they went, whatever you do, *stay put!* The group will soon be finding you from both the rear and the front. You can then chew out the rider who was responsible for you at that intersection!

The leader is also the first rider to meet oncoming traffic. When that happens, the leader should signal to everyone in the oncoming group (motorized or non-motorized) how many riders are behind him. He should signify the number with the fingers on his left (non-throttle) hand. Each successive rider in your group should do the same, each one signaling one less finger, until the sweep gives the 0 signal or "end" signal (cut across throat) to indicate he is the last rider in the group. Of course to perform this correctly, each rider needs to be aware how many riders are behind him or her in line.

HAND SIGNALS
Follow the rider in front of you at a safe distance, just like you would with a car on the highway. Keep in mind that there are all sorts of obstacles that can pop up on trails that make riders hit the brakes quite often. One thing a rider can do to alert others is to raise his or her left hand up in the air to signal to the rider behind that they are slowing or stopping or that there is a big obstacle ahead.

Many trails actually have stop signs at various intersections. Always raise your hand when slowing for a stop sign. Many trail riders also give hand signals for turns at intersections similar to what we used as kids on bicycles (straight out for a left turn; a 90-degree L-shape for a right). These signals really make the novices in your group feel comfortable that someone is looking out for them.

Some states and communities actually allow riders to legally operate their ATVs on public roads (either limited or unlimited), and some ATVs are even licensed to ride on the street (with some modifications such as turn signals, tires, etc).

BUILDING A BETTER TRAIL QUAD
FINDING THE RIGHT SETUP FOR YOU

Chapter 6

HERE WE WILL COVER

- Better traction
- Handling more cargo
- Better protection
- Boosting vehicle comfort
- Better breathing
- Setting up the suspension
- Cheap and easy performance tips
- What's the story on pump gas?
- Things to pack for long adventures

Long-distance, multi-day trail rides require a lot of add-on accessories. Fortunately there are a ton of packs, boxes, and other cargo-hauling devices to choose from.

TIP

WHAT'S THE STORY ON PUMP GAS?

Some ATVs run better with different types of fuel. Sport and high-performance ATVs usually work better with super unleaded because the octane level is higher. The higher the octane level, the faster the combustion will be. Your engine will stay cleaner, and the performance will be at its peak. With utility and sport/utility-type quads, regular gas is fine because they are built to utilize a lower octane level.

It seems as though Americans have been customizing their vehicles for as long as bicycles, cars, motorcycles, and ATVs have been around. Many of us aren't completely happy with the way our machines come off the showroom floor, and want our vehicles to run a little faster, ride a little smoother, handle tougher terrain, or haul more cargo.

For the ATV trail rider, many products are available that can accomplish these things. Here's a closer look at some of the things available for the recreational trail rider who is intent on transforming his ATV into a better ride.

TIRES AND TRACTION

Switching to a different type of tire is one of the most common things riders do to their quads. The stock tires found on your quad are generally designed as all-around tires, providing good traction, wear, and comfort in nearly all types of terrain. As the stock tires wear out and riders become more familiar with the typical conditions and types of trails

they frequent, they may want to opt for a more specialized tire.

Basically, there are four different types of specialized tires: sand, mud, racing, and desert. Sand tires feature large paddles on an otherwise smooth tire and can be categorized into two different types—one for straight-ahead drag racing and the much more popular models, which are designed for sliding and turning as well as straight-ahead traction. Most riders stick with the stock front tires that do a fine job for playing around in the sand, but there are also front sand tires available that feature a single or double-rib down the middle for traction while turning.

Mud tires feature big lugs on a high-profile carcass and they work great in even the nastiest mudbogs. However, the real aggressive mud tires give the ATV a somewhat bumpy ride and heavier steering while on hard-packed surfaces. In addition, the really big lug tires are getting outlawed at more and more riding areas, as they cause more wear and tear on trails compared to a less radical design.

Motocross racing tires are generally flatter and low-profile, with evenly spaced knobbies. They are designed to get maximum traction and provide good bite on a variety of dirt surfaces from wet to hard pack. Many sport-quad trail riders opt for a similar tire so they can blaze down the trails at maximum velocity. Desert tires are similar, but feature a tall profile and tough sidewalls so they can handle all the high-speed hits they'll be taking from rocks.

Contrary to what you might think, a really good mud tire may not work very well in deep snow. A tire with too much grip will just dig you deeper in the snow, but in the mud, the aggressive traction of that same tire will hook up on a rut and provide just enough grip to get you out of a bad situation. For deep snow, look instead for a tire that features a less aggressive tread. If your winter trail riding includes ice-covered lakes and streams, you may want to add some small sheet metal screws to the knobs for extra traction on the glare ice. Riders who compete in ATV racing add lots of screws to their tires, but for general trail riding you may only need three or four dozen on each tire. Check them regularly after every ride as they tend to get torn out now and then.

For serious, deep-wood outings, a 6-plyrated carcass will be able to resist impacts on razor sharp rocks. On that type of tire, the sidewalls are much stiffer than a stock tire.

WHEELS

Choosing a good set of wheels is also essential, but should you choose steel or aluminum? There are such an array of styles on the market that it is sometimes difficult to make a choice.

A steel wheel is made of two parts, a stamped inner part, which is combined to a rolled outer rim. Both of these parts are welded together, and in some cases these parts are riveted together for more durability. The advantage of steel wheels is that you can paint them when they look bad and if there is a dent on one, you can hammer it back to its original look. The drawback is that you increase sprung weight, ultimately creating more stress on the drivetrain. Your ATV will have less power in acceleration, and you'll have to brake harder as well.

You might say that steel wheels add just a small amount of weight, but since the wheel is a dynamic part of the vehicle, the difference in inertia while in movement increases the load. It's part of the physical laws. There is a tremendous amount of force generated by movement, so you need more energy to accelerate and brake. This is why any added weight is so important.

Aluminum wheels are much lighter, less expensive, and they will not corrode like steel, but they are not as strong. There are two main types of aluminum wheels: rolled/spun and cast. Cast wheels tend to be heavier than spun wheels, but are still lighter than steel. They are in the midrange of the price scale. Cast wheels also are more dent resistant than spun, but they are more brittle: a big hit might just crack them.

One of the handiest things you can carry on your trail quad is a tow strap. The strap will be invaluable in the case of a breakdown and can help pull a quad out of the mud as well. Even better is an ATV equipped with an aftermarket winch (see Chapter 9 for more on winches).

Spun wheels tend to be more expensive, but are lighter and easier to repair than cast-aluminum wheels. There are many kinds of these high-performance racing wheel, some with reinforcing rings, or bead locks to keep the tire firmly in place.

MAKING YOUR QUAD INTO A REAL HAULER

Many of the new sport/utility quads, like the Bombardier, Polaris, and Arctic Cats models, provide impressive cargo space in the stock configuration. The multi-rack platform (MRP) system on the Arctic Cats and the lock-and-ride device on the Polaris ATVs are specifically designed for certain ATV applications, such as camping, hunting, or construction work.

There are tons of bolt-on or strap-on products made for ATVs that will increase cargo space and allow riders to carry specific items, such as guns, chainsaws, and shovels.

There are several different ways to carry extra fuel, the most obvious being to securely strap on some extra gas cans. This quad has a custom-built external fuel tank built around the rear grab bar. Some companies offer big, flat plastic auxiliary tanks that fit between the racks and the fenders.

Hunters can really trick out their quads if they want to. When you're out in the woods, you'd better make sure you remember where you park a camo quad!

The various components include rack extenders, drop baskets (which drop down at the back of the ATV to carry long items like rakes and shovels), zip-up cargo bags, and trunks. Some of the cargo bags and most of the trunks are fairly waterproof.

PROTECTING THE UNDERSIDE

Riders who are especially rough on their machines, such as those that tackle rocky trails and big mud bogs, need more protection for the underbelly. On most sport/utility quads, the manufacturers have installed some polymer (plastic) plates to protect the belly of the ATV. They are light, but they have a limited lifetime, especially if you're scraping over giant boulders. If the rock gets through and damages the bottom of your engine or transmission, you'll be looking at a big repair bill.

For most recreational ATVs, you should use skid plates that are fabricated from 5/32-inch (.160) 5052 H-32 aluminum. They'll provide enough protection if you are not too hard on your unit. For the bigger quads, like the Grizzly, Rincon, and Rubicon, you should go for a thicker plate, made from at least 3/16-inch (.190) aluminum. As for swingarm skid plates, the

One of the cheapest and easiest ways to getting more power out of your ATVs engine is to install a better breathing air filter.

TIP

AN ANCHOR CAN SAVE THE DAY

You might get stuck in the middle of a muddy field with no trees to attach your winch cable to. So it's always a good idea to bring a small boat anchor. They're designed to dig in the sand, or in the case of northern riders, snow and ice. When force is applied, an anchor may provide just enough grip to get you out of a tricky situation.

One thing almost every ATV rider is looking for is more traction. The easiest way to achieve that goal is to install a new set of tires. The tires that come stock on your quad are made for general-purpose use, but you can buy aftermarket tires that are designed to work best in specific conditions, such as mud, hardpack, sand, etc.

CHEAP AND EASY PERFORMANCE TIPS
LITTLE WAYS TO MAKE A BETTER TRAIL QUAD

• In cold weather use a lower-grade type of oil, such as 5w30. The less thick it is, the less stress on the mechanical components at the heart of your machine. In hot temperatures, you can increase to 20w50 grade. In the heat, the thicker the viscosity, the more it will protect your engine.

• Bring a small compressor or air tank with you so you can change your tire pressure. In sand or mud, reduce pressure to increase the footprint of the tire to the ground for better traction and floatation (digs in less). On rocky terrain you'll want increased pressure to get the best traction and avoid flats.

• Synthetic oils are better for engine life since they lose their viscosity at a slower rate. This type of oil is generally more expensive, but it keeps its performance under heat or cold weather, plus it will genuinely increase the performance of the engine.

• For trail riders with sport or high-performance quads, you can have more torque simply by going down one tooth on the countershaft sprocket or adding three on the rear sprocket. With these tweaks, you'll have better acceleration coming out of corners. You'll loose a little top speed, but hey, how much top speed do you need on the trail? I prefer a good acceleration when I come out of a mud hole.

• Don't forget to lubricate your chain; otherwise it will wear faster, and you risk damaging your motor if it breaks at high speed.

• Clean your ATV after a ride—don't wait for the mud to dry. A clean ATV makes it easier to spot leaking fluids, and you'll help retain the value of your machine when you want to sell it.

• Take some riding lessons. You'll be surprised at how you can gain speed just with a few basic riding techniques. If you're an advanced rider, try taking a class from a pro; they may be less expensive than you think.

• Change the cam (or cams, depending on your model) at a reasonable cost, and you'll feel a big difference in power.

For utility ATVs, install a lift kit to gain some ground clearance. It's inexpensive and the ground clearance will be better.

Nearly all ATV motocross racers use nerf bars as extra protection for their foot area. If you are into play racing with your buddies, you may want to consider a set for your sport or high-performance machine.

standard thickness is 3/16 of an inch (.190).

For high-performance sport quads, you should use 1/4-inch (.250) 6061-T6 extruded aluminum with a long-wearing integral chain guide. They won't add too much weight to your ATV, and you'll have good protection. You can install your skid plates easily using either the stock mounts or some tough heat-treated chrome-moly steel clamps or a combination of both.

Plastic skid plates are light. They won't rust and will not deform on impact. They also create less noise when you're riding on a rocky terrain, and they slide better on an obstacle, but they don't compare in terms of full protection of the vital components of your quad.

BETTER COMFORT IN THE COLD

You'll enjoy winter riding if you put on the proper equipment like a heated thumb throttle and heated handgrips. Kimpex and Parts Unlimited both offer this type of equipment. You can also leave them installed on your quad in the summertime, as they come in handy on cool mornings. Once the day warms up, you can cut the power to the grips by pressing two small buttons.

You'll enjoy winter riding if you put on the proper equipment like a heated thumb throttle and heated handgrips.

Installing your own is not necessarily an easy task. It might be something you want your dealer to do since a bad installation can result in a fire, or you could burn your hands if they heat up too much.

Heated grips work by way of a wire that is connected to the battery via a fuse, sending power to small heaters that are put inside the grips. They take about five minutes to heat

This is taking the cargo box to the extreme. Just think of all the stuff you could easily and securely pack in something this big.

TIP

CHANGING GRIPS

Before sliding replacement grips on the handlebar, spray some hairspray inside the grips and on the handlebar. It helps them slip on and once the grips are installed, the hairspray will dry, and the grips won't turn or come slack on the handlebar.

There are a variety of handguards available to protect you from the cold, rain, and branches.

up and two settings are available—medium or hot.

Another way to keep your hands warm while riding quads is to install some handguards. They not only protect you from the cold, but also from branches and roost from rider in front of you. There are also grip mitts that slide over your whole control assembly. For riders who prefer thinner gloves for better feeling on the controls, these are the way to go.

Windshields are practical since they provide better protection from the wind or debris. They are readily available through aftermarket. A good quality windshield is made from a clear, high-quality polycarbonate (Lexan) that creates less distortion. The only inconvenience of having one is that when you are riding on bumpy trails and standing up on your machine, the windshield gets in the way of your chin. The higher the windshield, the better the comfort in rain or when following someone on a dusty trail. The drawback is that when there is a strong wind, you'll feel some pushing on the handlebars.

Windshields are relatively easy to install, and they come with special brackets for the handlebar. Make sure the brackets are secured

to the faring because the vibration caused by your ATV might unscrew the fasteners. Also, always be careful when cleaning the windshield, since they scratch easily; use some light soap and water before rubbing.

BETTER BREATHING FOR YOUR ENGINE

One important way to maximize power for your quad is to install an aftermarket air filter. Once you increase the airflow, you gain acceleration and horsepower. You should also install a pre-filter with your air filter.

This is an especially good move if you like to play in water or in a very dusty environment. When you play in water, the water turns into steam once it touches a hot engine and then that steam is sucked directly into the air box. It can cause your motor to sputter and may also make the engine run rich. This will become worse if you run with the lid off. With an outerwear pre-filter, mud and water won't go through the engine when you dive too quickly into water and create a splash. Instead, water will be directed into the bottom of the air box and down through the water-plug hole. It's the best way to protect your engine without sacrificing airflow.

THINGS TO PACK ON LONG ATV ADVENTURES
YOU'LL BE GLAD YOU DID

For really long adventures into the back country, ATV riders should pack more than the usual tool kit, extra spark, and spare water. The following is a list of things you may want to consider taking along on your next outing:

- GPS
- Cell phone
- Multi-tool, including knife
- Heavy-duty flashlight
- Duct tape
- 25 feet of rope with a tow hook
- Chemical light sticks
- First-aid kit
- Roll of stove wire (for repairs)
- Thermal blanket
- Fire starter
- Water purifier
- Insect repellent

- Compact flare gun
- Disposable lighter
- 12x12-foot orange plastic tarp (doubles as a groundsheet during repairs and a shelter)
- Tire repair kit (including tire plugs and tool, a pump or CO_2 canisters with
- valve adapter)
Spare transmission belt (for automatics)

Tools
- Multi-bit screwdriver
- Small hatchet
- Wrench set
- Socket wrench set
- Extra spark plugs
- Folding saw
- Vise-Grips

Once you increase the airflow, you gain acceleration and horsepower. You should also install a pre-filter with your air filter.

SETTING THE SUSPENSION

Many recreational and sport/utility four-wheelers feature adjustable shocks. With these, you can adjust the preload (the amount of tension on the shock springs) to your style of riding, or if you're carrying a lot of cargo. Shocks on most recreational-type quads typically have five-way settings, each one making the shock's action slightly stiffer. A special tool (spanner wrench) is provided inside most ATV toolboxes to make the setting change.

If your quad has a tendency to tilt to the side during cornering and braking, especially if you are an aggressive rider, simply add more preload to the front shocks to make the shock's action stiffer. If your racks are full and heavy, you need to make the same adjustments to keep your ATV from squatting and losing ground clearance.

On sport and high-performance quads, there are more choices when it comes to setting your shocks. You can change the preload, damping, and rebound settings. This usually only takes a few minutes. A

slower rebound means your shock will be slower in snapping back to its full stroke, so the quad will have less of a tendency to bounce back towards you after a landing. The faster the rebound, the quicker the shock will travel in its stroke, so the rear end will usually kick on bumps.

Rebound is when the shock is going back up in its stroke, but what about compression damping, what does it do? Compression damping controls how fast the suspension will compress when you hit a bump. The more damping you use, the slower the shock will compress. If you use a lot of damping and you go over large jumps, the suspension will not bottom out and you'll have better control. The downside is that the suspension will feel much harder for you when you go through small bumps. You are the only one that can determine how much damping you want; it's all a question of your type of riding and the type of terrain you are playing on.

Always take the time to adjust and readjust to your needs. You'll be surprised how much your ride can change.

TIP

REJET WHEN YOU CHANGE PIPES

If you plan on installing a pipe without rejetting, you'll be disappointed to find that in most cases your quad will lose performance. You need to get a full kit and rejet for maximum performance. (See Chapter 8 for more on jetting.)

BUILDING AN ATV WORKHORSE

THERE'S A WHOLE LOT OF CHORES TO BE DONE

HERE WE WILL COVER
• **Farming and ranching**
• **Hunting**
• **Camping**
• **Construction**
• **Patrol and rescue**
• **Pull-behind trailers**

Pull-behind trailers increase the carrying capacity of ATVs considerably.

Many manufacturers, including Swisher, Cycle Country, Kunz, and B-I-H Enterprises, now design ATV implements that produce big-time results in the agricultural market.

ATVs are purchased for two main reasons: for recreation and for work. In fact, of all the units currently being sold every year, more than half of the riders use them primarily for utility purposes. That means hunters, fishermen, farmers, ranchers, and work-related riders are a large percentage of the ATV public.

Riders can add tons of aftermarket items to make their quad perform specific chores. Today it seems like someone has invented a way to attach just about any device to the front, rear, or top of quad to get a job done—be it plowing snow, mowing grass, hauling trailers, planting seeds, fertilizing crops, or even making your quad into a mobile ice fishing shack!

FARMING AND RANCHING

Many farmers and ranchers use utility four-wheelers to pull trailers and wagons, move and feed livestock, mow and clear land, and spend lots of time simply using it as cheap and easy transportation from Point A to Point B.

Many manufacturers, including Swisher,

Cycle Country, Kunz, and B-I-H Enterprises, now design ATV implements that produce big-time results in the agricultural market. Swisher makes an excellent fence row mower that actually swings under an electric wire fence, cutting weeds and grass that can short out electric fencing. Several companies produce both commercial-grade finish mowers and rough-cut brush hogs for mowing up to a 60-inch swath. Many of these units are built to the highest standards and hold up to years of use.

Some of the most exciting of all products come in the Groundbuster product line from B-I-H Enterprises. These ATV planting implements include the Ground Buster planting unit and the Ground Pulverized Lime Spreader. The planting unit consists of two sets (front and rear) of 18-inch heavy-duty disc blades that are easily adjustable (up to 30-degree angle) for aggressive cutting. The unit is equipped with electric lift, culti-packer, grading mat, and broadcast spreader, and it comes with both a single-point hitch (for use with ATVs)

Using a basic utility workhorse quad to help feed livestock, haul supplies, or clear land is common in ranching operations.

Using your ATV to set up remote campsites is an absolute joy. Arctic Cat makes a unique Multi-Rack Platform Speedrack system that features 40 different accessory attachments, some of which are designed specifically for camping equipment.

Go to any local sprint car or midget race and you'll find all sorts of custom-built pit ATVs. Since those kinds of race cars have no onboard starters like stock cars, ATVs are used to push them out to the starting line.

and a three-point hitch (for use with tractors). The lime spreader is a ground-driven implement that features an opening gate that dispenses lime evenly, getting the soil's pH levels to the right configuration for planting.

HUNTING

Quads have become popular among hunters for two main reasons: ATVs are quite handy for transporting the hunter and his equipment to and from the field and they can help haul a kill out of the woods.

Surveys have shown the typical hunting ATV to be a 400cc utility ATV with several accessories, such as a gun scabbard, bow/tree stand carrier, and rack bags for clothing and gear. Of course, individual needs and ATV applications vary with geographical areas as with hunting situations. Southern wet regions may use

Many hunters have replaced their pack horses with ATVs.

more aggressive aftermarket tires for traction in wet, muddy conditions, and in farther north in colder climates, ATV enclosures are often used in tough weather conditions.

Beyond the actual hunting trip, it's now common for groups of hunters to use ATVs as small farm tractors, often planting a "crop" to attract their game. These hunters use small pull-behind ATV farming implements to soil, lime, fertilize, and plant very effective small food plots. Working ATVs don't stop there, though; they also help with jobs such as building tree stands, placing feed, and posting property lines.

CAMPING

Could there a better way to travel deep into the wilderness for a camping trip than in the saddle of your ATV? But when you load your four-wheeler up with overnight equipment, your machine really gets a workout.

Thankfully, there are plenty of ways to increase your machine's usefulness when preparing for a camping adventure. First off,

check out what accessory manufacturers are offering in this field. For one, you might want to consider increasing your rack capacity. Dropdown racks are a great way to carry extra containers of water, gas, or food. Also, several companies produce flat water and fuel containers that lay flat on the racks and other items can be strapped down on top of these containers for maximum rack loading capacity. Some riders will also use a pull-behind ATV cargo trailer to carry their stuff. One that is 3x6 feet would be plenty big enough to carry coolers, cook stoves, tents, and water or fuel containers.

If camping and riding is a top priority for you, you may want to consider buying a Jumping Jack trailer. These units are a combination of a popup camper and a transport unit for your ATV. The trailer itself is a metal-framed unit with expanded steel throughout its larger panels. This framework is opened on top and supported with the main portion of the trailer to create a popup-based platform.

Inside is a heavy-rubber bag, which can

One of the most popular chores ATVs are used for in the northern climes is snow plowing. A 4x4 quad works best with these big easily removable snowplows.

TIP

CARGO WEIGHT MAKES A DIFFERENCE

First-time ATV owners should know that any time weight is placed in or on your ATV racks, it will affect the vehicle's performance. By loading up ATV racks with farming, hunting, or search and rescue accessories, your quad will have a higher center of gravity and thus handle differently. You can help the handling by stiffening up the re-load settings on the front and rear shocks. Always check your ATVs load capacity before filling it up with equipment, and don't go over the limits.

HITTING THE TRAIL
FINDING THE TRAILER THAT'S RIGHT FOR YOUR ATV

When looking to use a trailer with your four-wheeler, you always have to consider first what you'll be using the pull-behind for.

For example, if you want to do yard work, such as hauling leaves, grass clippings, and garden tools, you can make do with a light-duty steel or plastic ATV trailer.

When it comes to heavy-duty loads, operators need to look for a specialty trailer with a large weight limit, proper tires, axles, and construction.

Most ATV riders use ATV trailers for hauling firewood or moving dirt, rocks, lime, and fertilizer. All of these are heavy objects, so

when hauling them, ATV operators should have them evenly loaded in their trailers. The weight should also not be placed at the far front or back of the trailer.

You also should keep in mind that pulling a weighted trailer will affect the way your ATV operates. If going down hill, that extra weight will push your ATV, making braking more difficult. Going uphill, a weighted trailer causes more drag.

No matter what you're doing, you should always keep your quad below its towing capacity. This is detailed in your owner's manual.

For riders who need to navigate really extreme terrain for their work, there are a couple of companies that offer track systems similar to what is found on tanks and caterpillars. The ride is slow and rough, but they certainly get through the really nasty stuff better than an ATV with tires!

be unzipped to release a complete canvas tent. The camper unit can be set up in less than five minutes and comes with plenty of options, including an outside sink, water

supply jug, and rain-fly front. When you walk inside the camper, you will notice two side beds with comfortable padded top mats and a warm rugged floor. The unit uses the

tailgate as a step up to enter. This also is a great place to keep your boots and gear off the ground.

This trailer is also easily converted into a purebred utility workhouse trailer. First, drop the tailgate and place the flat-top portions in the upright positions. Then slide the rubber tent bag out from inside the trailer and you're ready to work. When you return, just have a friend help you slide the tent bag back inside and you're ready for the next trip.

When you decide you're ready to go, Jumping Jack supplies a set of ramps to load your ATVs on top of the trailer itself. These are an optional item, but make the job quite easy.

CONSTRUCTION
Two big manufacturers have started producing ATVs made specifically for the construction or building field. Arctic Cat produces the MRP system (multi-rack platform) that is an open-channel receiver rack for front and rear, specifically designed to accept 25 different slide-on accessory racks

and specialty items. These accessories racks can be changed very easily with pull pins and used front or back interchangeably. Users may select from six different applications—fishing, camping, big game hunting, construction, waterfowl, and farming and ranching. So in just a few minutes, a construction worker can change his quad from a work-related setup to a recreational fishing vehicle.

Polaris also has a specialty construction line in its Ranger series. The construction-type, side-by-side cargo units are offered in a bright yellow color and are speed sensitive and controlled by two different starting key types. Controlling the speed helps increase the safety of these units. The Rangers (and all Polaris Sportsman ATVs) are also compatible with the Lock & Ride system. This system enables users to easily secure accessories and fit into holes in the utility box of the Ranger. The highlight of the new system is Expanding Anchor Technology. The rider drops an expanding plug into the pre-drilled holes in the machine, and simply pushes the handle down to lock the accessory in place. The

One of the most popular excuses for the man of house to buy a new quad is "but Honey, I can take care of the lawn with it." And, after buying a pull-behind mower, he *can* keep his promise!

TIP

THE ULTIMATE IN TRACTION
If you're really doing some heavy-duty hauling, or are working in an area with loose terrain, your ATV may need the ultimate in traction. Several companies offer ATV track system that works on the same design basis as a military tank track. By no means are these tracks cheap (nor is the ride very comfortable or as fast), but there is a substantial increase in traction and ground clearance under the vehicle when you use them.

An incredible number of people use ATVs for hunting. Though there are mixed feelings about this practice (even with other hunters), there are a lot of accessories available to make an ultimate hunting quad. For more on the rules and ethics of using your ATV for hunting, see Chapter 5.

accessories are a perfect fit and are rattle-free. Available accessories include a sprayer, cargo box, and gun scabbard.

Lastly, Arctic Cat and Polaris manufacture standard utility ATV models with cargo boxes incorporated into the back of the ATV. These units are handy for carrying tools and building materials.

PATROL AND RESCUE

The ATV supplies several advantages over the typical truck or jeep-style vehicle in rescue operations. For one, the short wheelbase of an ATV gives riders the ability to traverse canyons, ridges, open fields and grasslands, as well as brush-lined areas. The ATV search-and-rescue concept also works well in areas with large trail systems.

Using ATVs in rescue has become so popular in fact that Hocking College, in Nelsonville, Ohio, now offers an ATV search and rescue course. Other than police departments, forest service officials, and emergency response personnel, several ATV clubs now have become involved in ATV rescues.

Other agencies have found uses for rescue ATVs as well. Security guards and customs and border patrol all see ATVs as necessary in their job efforts. In fact, the

Hatfield and McCoy Trail system, in West Virginia, has sheriff's deputies patrolling its 500-plus miles of ATV trails on quads. These deputies have offices at each trailhead and can respond more quickly by riding their four-wheeler to the spot where they are needed.

Now this looks like fun! Use your ATV to get all your ice fishing gear out onto your favorite lake. Just make sure the ice is thick enough to handle the weight of your quad or you may be fishing for it come spring.

Other than police departments, forest service officials, and emergency response personnel, several ATV clubs now have become involved in ATV rescues.

Many search and rescue operations utilize ATVs to get folks in and out of rough terrain.

Chapter 8

BUILDING A FASTER, MORE POWERFUL ATV ENGINE
PUTTING TOGETHER AN ALL-TERRAIN HOT ROD

HERE WE WILL COVER

- **Air intake and exhaust**
- **Carburetors and cams**
- **Porting and headwork**
- **Pistons and big-bore kits**
- **Stroker kits and black boxes**
- **Jetting and fuel**
- **Superchargers and turbochargers**

Many ATV riders aren't satisfied with their machines in stock form. So they often modify their engine so their ATV has more zip on the track and trail.

When looking at intake modifications, you're simply trying to get more air/fuel mixture into the engine more quickly.

Hopping up ATV engines is a big business, with hundreds of performance shops located throughout the country. There are all sorts of ways to coax more power from your stock engine and hopefully you'll make the right decisions, as some the modifications can be quite costly. The modifications you choose depend on what type of power increase you're looking for. Some mods add more to the low end of the rpm power curve (trail riders who do extreme terrain like this), while others focus more on the midrange (a favorite of motoross and cross-country racers). Flat-track and short-track racers usually seek top-end rpm power.

AIR INTAKE MODIFICATIONS

When looking at intake modifications, you're simply trying to get more air/fuel mixture into the engine more quickly. The quick-and-easy method of increasing air flow into an engine is to simply remove the air box lid. This gives unlimited airflow to the filter element. However, it has a big downside in that it also

gives unrestricted access to dirt, mud, and water. If your riding conditions require you to be in the mud or water, this option obviously has its drawbacks. Yet if you're going to be riding in reasonably dry conditions, the benefits far outweigh the drawbacks; however, you should be cleaning your filter after every ride now.

The air box's air filter element is also a critical part of this formula. The ideal element structure should have sufficient surface area to prevent particulate matter clogging and be easily cleanable. And most importantly, there should be as little flow restriction as possible. Currently, one of the best high-performance filter elements for the above type of high-flow sealed air box is the K&N type of pleated, oiled cotton gauze. If you just plan to remove your air box lid, using a K&N type in conjunction with one of the synthetic pre-filter sock covers will reduce the chance of water entry. For dry conditions, especially sand, the oiled foam element is a great choice. Paper-type filter elements have no place off-road at all.

Show and go. Hopped up quads not only go faster, but they look cooler, too!

Aftermarket high-performance exhaust pipes are one of the easiest ways to add horsepower to your machine. This fat two-stroke pipe utilizes the exhaust pulse to pull the spent gasses out, thereby sucking in a stronger air/fuel charge.

Remember to properly oil the filter element according to the manufacturer's recommendations. A dry element will provide minimal stoppage of foreign matter. It is the filter oil that does the work. Remember to use the correct type of filter oil for each type of filter element. They are not interchangeable. And never substitute anything other than filter oil for re-oiling the elements. Regular motor oil and the like will settle towards the bottom of the filter element, saturating it, leaving the top of the element dry and exposed to dirt entry. Oils made specifically for filters will stay in "suspension" within the element's body to provide the best filtering capability.

PERFORMANCE EXHAUSTS

The goal of an exhaust is to rid the engine of the spent gasses with as little restriction as possible. This allows the efficient refilling of the cylinder with a fresh fuel/oil mixture. A properly designed performance exhaust system will use the power of the exhaust, as well as its audio signature, to increase power by not only creating a vacuum outside the exhaust port to aid in gas extraction, but to "supercharge" the cylinders incoming mixture.

When looking at a high-performance exhaust, for either a two- or four-stroke engine, you have to decide what type of riding you will be doing with this pipe. Pipes are basically designed to add low-end, mid-range, or top-end power. Manufacturers may even provide a dyno chart comparing stock to modified. Be sure to check closely for what additional modifications were done when the

Riders who are into sand dragging perform lots of engine mods to get the best launch off the line. They also like to use a lengthened swingarm to eliminate wheelies.

dyno was run (i.e., air box modifications, increased jetting).

OK, so just how is a mid-range or top-end pipe determined? In a four-stroke engine, this has to do with the diameter of the headpipe as well as its length. The larger the headpipe diameter is, the more power that can be produced—up to a point. The longer the pipe, the more low- to mid-range bias. Conversely, a shorter pipe tends to allow a motor to rev higher and produce more top-end power. In a two-stroke, the diameter and length of the expansion chamber (they look much fatter than four-stroke pipe) determine the exhaust's range.

A quiet performance muffler generally is larger than a full-on race muffler. The noise signature must be absorbed by muffler packing or dampened by baffles while still allowing relatively unrestricted outflow to maintain power.

Whether you're installing a high-performance pipe on a two- or four-stroke engine, you should rejet the carburetor for maximum performance. The pipe manufacturer usually will provide the right jetting specs for your particular model.

BIGGER CARBURETORS

A larger carburetor can provide a dramatic increase in an engine's power output, or it can create an unmanageable beast. It all has to do with the venturi size. As the airflow passes into the carburetor's venturi, the airflow speed

is increased. For a carburetor to function properly, there must be a certain airflow speed for efficient introduction of fuel into the mixture. Go below that threshold and fuel atomization is not efficient. Bigger carbs usually work best with intake and pipe mods, and perhaps an increase in displacement.

The larger the carburetor, the higher the revs have to be. If you plan on maintaining higher revs and can keep the air flow speed high with a stock bore or plan on increasing displacement, then a larger carburetor can definitely flow more mixture into the combustion chamber, creating an increase in power from upper mid-range to top-end with stock displacement. Or if you increase the displacement by either boring or stroking, then a larger carburetor can increase power.

One caveat to the above, in a motor with documented undersized intake ports, an increase in carburetor size can produce power everywhere, including low end with a stock bore.

CAMS

Cams can radically change how an engine responds to throttle input. In a four-stroke engine, a cam is the valve controller. The valves open when the intake lobe of the cam either forces a rocker arm to push down on a valve stem or the lobe acts directly on a lifter bucket. Typically to increase power, the intake valves are opened a few degrees earlier, kept open longer, and opened deeper. An exhaust valve is generally kept open longer and deeper.

How the valves are opened control the type of power a cam produces. Cams with a longer duration (valve opening time in degrees) tend to provide more revs and top-end power. Cams with more valve lift (valves open deeper) tend to produce more torque and mid-range power.

Changing the valve timing will cause the valves to be in close proximity to the piston. In some cases, especially with the more radical cams, there will be an interference with the piston. The valves hitting the piston will cause damage to the valves requiring replacement. To alleviate this problem, pistons can either be relieved by increasing the size of the valve cutouts in the top of the piston or a new piston can be purchased that has the increased clearance already there. Most stock pistons

Painting the plastic on quads is tricky business and requires special pre-coats and final clear coats. You still have to worry about the paint cracking if the fenders get bent. But it sure does look good!

Cams can radically change how an engine responds to throttle input. In a four-stroke engine, a cam is the valve controller.

You can take just about any ATV part to a professional metal coating company and have it chromed, even an entire engine!

TIP

NIKASIL COATING FOR HIGH-PERFORMANCE ENGINES

A typical ATV engine has a cast-iron cylinder sleeve pressed into the center of an aluminum cylinder. Some high-performance engines dispense with the cast-iron sleeve and have a plasma spray, Nikasil, added onto the aluminum walls. Nikasil is a nickel and silicon carbide matrix coating. The nickel matrix itself is very hard, providing a very long-wearing surface.

Throughout the nickel matrix are particles of silicon carbide, which are extremely hard and form a matrix of spots in which oil can collect. The silicon carbide particles contribute to longer engine life by providing good cylinder lubrication. A Nikasil layer generates less friction than a comparable cast-iron liner, allowing the motor to rev faster, thus increasing acceleration and overall power.

---

have enough valve clearance to tolerate a "mild" or mid-range cam.

When deciding on a replacement camshaft, remember that only a few degrees more duration or a few thousandths of an inch more lift can have a dramatic effect on the way an engine responds to throttle and produces power. Generally the average consumer tends to purchase too "hot" a cam. That is one with too much lift or duration. Unless you have a specific purpose for this engine, you should

look at a "mild" or mid-range cam. A mid-range cam coupled with other engine modifications will yield the most satisfactory results and will be the easiest to ride with the least amount of rider work.

TWO-STROKE PORTING

A two-stroke cylinder has cutouts in the cylinder wall where fuel is admitted and exhaust is removed. By adjusting the height and width of these ports, the power characteristics of the

There are even aftermarket cylinders available for some models. These were very popular with the Honda FourTrax 250R two-stroke model since riders were still racing them 10 years after the ATV disappeared from showroom floors.

DEFINITION

Supercharging: This process forces air into the carburetor with an engine-powered blower. With this added volume of air being forced into the engine, the carburetor can add a much larger amount of fuel to the mixture, creating a large increase in power. The advantages of supercharging include having a more responsive engine because the blower's speed is directly connected to the speed of the crankshaft. The downside is that the compression ratio of the engine either has to be lowered or the boost pressure of the supercharger has to be cut back to prevent the motor from overheating.

Typically, 5 to 8 psi of boost is used with normal compression ratios and 10 psi or more of boost is used with pistons having a lowered compression ratio in the 6–8:1 range.

engine can be changed. Generally raising the exhaust port, decking the piston at both TDC (top dead center) and BDC (bottom dead center), and modifying the head volume for more cranking pressure will produce an increase in usable power with most engines.

However, the chances an average person could do the required work with a "Dremel" is not good. This is a job for a professional engine tuner. Remember to specify to your tuner what type of power you require when he asks. If he

does not inquire, take your cylinder elsewhere! He should also ask for your head and piston, too. If he does not, then just walk away. All these pieces are necessary for a quality "port" job.

FOUR-STROKE HEAD WORK

The head of a four-stroke motor is where power can either be won or lost. Porting here consists of smoothing and adjusting the heads intake and exhaust port angles to promote increased flow with fewer restrictions. Then

Along with engine modifications, many ATV racers utilize aftermarket swingarms, shocks, and axles to improve the performance of the suspension and handling characteristics.

Unless you are a racer, stick to a compression ratio that can survive on pump gas. Your piston maker can advise you as to how high you can go.

the valves may be contoured for increased flow. Rocker arms, if used, can be lightened or modified to allow a cam with more lift. Also the valve guide may need to be shortened if the cam's lift is great enough to interfere with the standard length guide or it interferes with flow.

Having a head ported for more flow is recommended when there are heat problems from increased displacement. The added flow potential cools down the head.

As with the two-stroke cylinder, a head can be quickly ruined by the untrained hand.

Let the proven professionals do it.

PISTONS

There are two types of pistons: forged and cast. Most OEM pistons are cast while most high-performance pistons are forged. Forged pistons have two to three times the strength and heat dissipation of cast pistons.

As discussed earlier, a high-performance four-stroke piston should have built-in valve-relief pockets. Four-stroke pistons have various compression ratios. On a two-stroke, the cylinder head must be modified to change the compression ratio. On some aftermarket two-stroke performance heads, the combustion chambers are replaceable parts and you can specify how many cubic centimeters of displacement you need.

With modern four-stroke engines, you can usually get away with going one point up on the compression ratio without going to special high octane race gas (e. g., from 10.0:1 to 11.0:1).

As the compression ratio goes up, so does the engine's efficiency. However, internal engine heat also rises. In the end, this comes down to a balancing act between power and melting the aluminum piston. Also as the compression ratio goes up, the need to keep detonation in check arises. So you then need a higher-octane fuel. Try 91 to 93 octane, and hope it stops the detonation. If not, then you will have to resort to purchasing race gas or an octane booster and mixing it with premium pump gas to raise the octane further. Unless you are a racer, stick to a compression ratio that can survive on pump

gas. Your piston maker can advise you as to how high you can go.

There are some other tricks to reduce detonation without the need for race gas. One is to install a more radical cam. This has the effect of depressing the compression pressure at lower rpm when there is more time for combustion, and that extra time can overheat the unburnt mixture. When you are "on the cam" and power is being produced in earnest, the rpm would be higher and the combustion in the cylinder would be occurring at a faster rate, hopefully too fast for the fuel to overheat and start to "ping."

The other thing to try is to make sure your mixture strength is rich enough. A slightly lean mixture will cause an already overheated motor to go off and detonate into destruction. The added fuel can cool the combustion chamber enough to get by.

BIG-BORE KITS

Increasing displacement is a sure way to increase horsepower. A big-bore kit consists

Different types of racing require different engine characteristics. The most popular form of ATV racing is motocross and those riders like an engine with a strong burst of mid-range power to get from corner to corner and to clear double jumps.

Aftermarket four-stroke pipes add power by increasing airflow through the engine. Unless you are only using your ATV for closed-course racing, you should buy a pipe that is designed to be nearly as quiet as stock. Loud ATVs are one of the biggest reasons riding areas are being shut down.

of a piston(s) with a larger diameter. With more piston surface area to be pushed by the combustion pressure comes pure torque. A moderate increase in piston diameter may be able to use the stock cylinder(s). If the cylinder sleeve wall thickness is too thin or a more aggressive bore kit is planned, new cylinder sleeves will need to be pressed into the cylinder.

When a larger piston is installed in an engine, the compression ratio can go up because the volume of the combustion chamber did not change, but the cylinder volume did (unless the bore-kit maker adjusted the pistons to bring back the ratio to stock levels). A higher ratio can mean additional heat or the need for a higher-octane rating—or both. Be sure to check the compression ratio of the larger pistons. That figure will take into account the change in cylinder volume.

The additional horsepower will produce extra engine heat too, which needs to be removed via water, air, or oil. A water-cooled engine usually can withstand an increase in heat, but the radiator fan may run more often.

Air-cooled engines can overheat if run slowly with not enough air passing over the engines fins. Increased oil temperatures can be handled by the addition of an accessory oil cooler or increasing the size of the factory-installed cooler.

Another downside to a bore kit is that the crankshaft balance can be thrown off with the added weight of the larger piston(s). This results in more vibration. It depends on the given motor as to just how much more vibration will be produced.

With the addition of a larger piston(s), the engines theoretical power-producing rpm limit will be lowered if all you do is install the bore kit. A larger displacement means that more air can be drawn into the motor. However with the same air box, intake tubes, carburetor(s), intake, cam(s), and exhaust, there are lots of flow restrictions that were not there before.

Now there is nothing wrong with just adding a bore kit; it can cure a stock engine that has a weak low-end or mid-range torque. However, if you do increase airflow with some of the other means discussed earlier, the

A finely-tuned ATV racing engine is a marvel of technology and it's rare to see any mechanical breakdowns in the powerplant during competition. It's a good thing too, considering the consequences of having a seized piston just before taking off on a jump like this.

engine can produce even more power from low end through top end.

STROKER KITS

Stroker kits increase displacement like a bore kit, yet they do not obtain the displacement through a larger bore. The increase in displacement is the result of a longer piston stroke. The connecting point for the pistons' connecting rod to the crank is moved further from the crankshaft's centerline. The connecting rod is then either shortened or replaced with a new rod. The new length is figured to keep the piston from traveling no higher than it did before, or it would hit the head.

Because the connecting rod is now further from the crankshaft's center, the piston can now travel further downward. This gives you the extra displacement. The piston is either modified or replaced with a new one that has shorter piston skirt to clear the crankshaft at BDC.

Engines that have been "stroked" produce more power everywhere and rev noticeably quicker than a stock engine. Unfortunately though, they will have the same heat and vibration problems associated with a big-bore kit. And there is a new problem with these: piston life. Because the piston is traveling further in the same period of time, the feet per minute (fpm) of the piston is higher than stock. This higher speed wears away at the piston skirt at an accelerated rate. Also because the stroker's piston has a shorter piston skirt, there is less surface area to stabilize the piston. It is best to gear higher

---

DEFINITION

Turbocharging: This process forces air into the carburetor with an exhaust-powered blower. With this added volume of air being forced into the engine, the carburetor can add a much larger amount of fuel to the mixture, creating a large increase in power. It works as the engine's exhaust is piped into a turbine that spins the intake blower.

The advantages of a turbocharged engine are increased power potential over a supercharged engine because there are no engine-associated power losses. The downside is poor throttle response because the turbocharger turbine only responds to exhaust volume increases. Also there is a loss of blower efficiency below about half throttle. At engine speeds below half, there is simply not enough exhaust volume to power the exhaust turbine. Like a supercharger on an ATV, the compression ratio of the engine either has to be lowered or the boost pressure of the turbocharger has to be cut back to prevent the motor from overheating.

Typically 5 to 8 psi of boost is used with normal compression ratios and 10 psi or more of boost is used with pistons having a lowered compression ratio in the 6–8:1 range.

Even sport/utility trail riders may enjoy a little added performance in the form of a pipe or a cam.

and/or upshift and use the engine's increased low- and mid-range torque, thus keeping the revs lower to maximize piston life.

A big-bore kit coupled with a stroker crank is the ultimate, providing you more power everywhere. All other modifications before this need to be done, and at this level are usually included in a professionally assembled package for maximum component reliability and performance.

IGNITION "BLACK BOXES"

With the addition of solid-state "electronic" ignitions, the home tuner has lost the ability to adjust the ignition system to any performance modifications. Luckily, the aftermarket has responded with replacement ignition modules commonly called "black boxes" because the early units were just that, black boxes. So the moniker has stuck in the world of motorsports.

What these replacement ignition-control units provide is a different ignition curve that works better with other high-performance modifications. Sometimes the aftermarket has discovered that the factory boxes did not do a good job of controlling a stock engine and that the addition of a different box will "wake up" the potential of a given stock engine.

HOP-UPS STEP-BY-STEP
IN WHAT ORDER SHOULD THE MODIFICATIONS BE?

Four-Stroke: Start with the intake modifications (air filter and air box). If you are happy, stop. If not, then add a pipe (performance exhaust). If you are happy, stop. After the intake mods and pipe installation, you could go for a cam at this time. And if the cam timing is not too radical, you can stick with the stock piston. A displacement increase can be next along with adding a bigger carb.

After you have the intake mods, pipe, and a displacement increase, porting the head is great way to reduce heat and increase flow. A black box may be the next step. It depends on the model as to whether it is worth the cost. The final step for serious drag racers would be forced air induction systems (e.g., supercharging and turbocharging).

Two-Stroke: Start with the intake modifications. If you are happy, stop. If not, then add a pipe. If you are happy, stop. If not, then consider several things at once. The next step would be to have the cylinder professionally ported, the head modified, and a high-performance forged piston installed. These three things should really be done at the same time. You can't do a proper porting job without the head being worked on for volume and cranking pressure and the piston is needed for decking.

Of course, at this time you could also consider a big-bore kit with the ported cylinder, forged piston, and headwork. The last thing you could do for serious horsepower is the stroker crank with or without a bore kit. This level requires everything else before it.

There is a common myth that all motors will run better on high-octane fuel. That's not true since high-octane fuels don't do anything for an engine that isn't already pinging. If you are at 91 to 93 octane pump gas and you are still experiencing detonation, then you will either need to use an octane booster or mix pump gas with race gas to raise the octane rating. If you really went crazy with the compression ratio on your race quad, then pure race gas will be necessary.

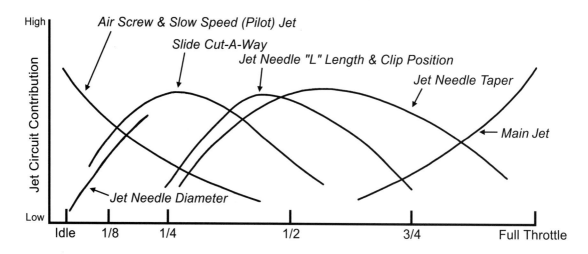

Replacement is as simple as disconnecting the electrical multi-connector and unbolting the old box and installing the new one. Rely on the manufacturer of the black box to tell you what performance modifications its box is set up for. Some black boxes are adjustable for a number of modifications and different rev limits.

JETTING

Most modifications to an ATV engine require a carburetor jetting change. Carb jets control the air/fuel mixtures at various throttle settings. Some components, such performance pipes, come with a "jet kit" made specifically for your ATV model. In many cases the jet kits will work fine, but if you have done other modifications that affect air intake, there may be some lean (not enough fuel) or rich (too much fuel) spots in your throttle settings and you'll have to perform the age-old jet ritual of a jetting check. While a motor can (and will) operate on a mixture that is considerably richer or leaner, power output falls off. If you happen to go leaner and ride it

Some components, such performance pipes, come with a "jet kit" made specifically for your ATV model.

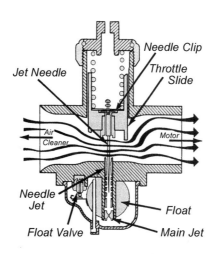

hard, you may end up with an over-heated motor, or worse, a seizure.

A VARIETY OF JETS

A carburetor has main and slow (pilot) jets that can be changed. The jet needle attached to the bottom of the slide is set at a certain height, so only the idle mixture screw is adjustable. If you have increased airflow as the result of modifications, the increased volume will still be mixed with the same amount of fuel as before, resulting in a lean mixture.

If you replace the main jet with a larger numbered jet, the jet's internal hole will be larger, thus flowing a greater quantity of fuel at three-fourths of full throttle. If you raise the position of the slide's jet needle by lowering the jet needle clip, you are allowing more fuel to rise out of the needle jet at a given part throttle position which is generally a fourth to three-fourths open. If you replace the low speed (pilot) jet with a larger numbered jet, the internal hole will be larger, thus flowing more fuel at very small openings of one-sixteenth to one-fourth throttle.

IDLE MIXTURE SCREW CAN BE TRICKY

The idle mixture screw is the only externally adjustable carburetor jet available and controls up to one-eighth throttle only. The first type of idle mixture screw is a fuel screw. It regulates the flow of fuel into the idle circuit. This type of screw is located ahead of the carb's slide tower (motor side) and is most often found under the carb's bore and upside-down directly ahead of the carb's float bowl. By turning the screw out, you increase the amount of fuel that is allowed to slip around the tapered needle and into the carb's bore.

If the idle mixture adjustment screw is located behind the carb's slide tower (air box side), then the adjusting needle regulates air flow into a fixed flow of fuel intended for idle. By turning this screw inward you are reducing the air flow, thus richening the idle mixture.

When the motor is up to operating temperature, set your idle speed screw to a stable idle. Then use either your idle fuel or air screw to obtain a stable idle. Reset the idle speed screw as necessary after obtaining the correct idle mixture.

MAIN JET

The main jet controls three-fourths-full throttle only. Ideally you should start very rich (large numbered jet) and test at full throttle. The engine should skip and blubber. If not, then you are not rich enough! Once you have your rich stumble, back off one size at a time until full throttle operation results in normal operation. (Note: If your ATV runs faster at three-fourths throttle than full throttle, you are definitely lean on the main!)

JET NEEDLE

The slide's jet needle controls one fourth to three-fourths throttle. If you have a soft hesitation, without a hard stumble, anywhere between one-fourth and three-fourths throttle, chances are your needle is lean, so raise the needle by lowering the clip. Conversely, if you have a hard stumble, chances are the needle position is rich, so lower the needle by raising the clip.

If you get very unlucky, you might have to start playing with jet needle taper, which controls how fast the mixture increases as the jet needle is raised. This would come into play if you were lean at one-fourth throttle, yet rich at three-fourths throttle. The length of the needle comes into play here, too. The diameter of the needle controls how much fuel escapes around the needle while still inside the needle jet. The larger the diameter of the straight section or "L" length, the leaner the mixture.

SLIDE CUTAWAY

The slide cutaway controls the amount of air allowed to pass under the slide at one-eighth to one-fourth throttle. It controls the transition from the low speed (pilot) jet to the main jet-fed needle jet/jet needle. Replacing

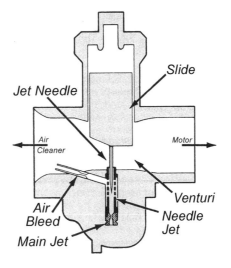

the slide with one that has a smaller number (less cut-a-way) will decrease the amount of airflow under the slide at one-eighth to one-fourth throttle openings, thus creating a richer mixture at that throttle opening. If you have a rich condition at one-eighth to one-fourth throttle and you can't go any leaner, try a smaller cut-a-way.

Thankfully, jet needle taper, diameter, "L" length, and slide cut-a-way are usually not affected by most simple pipe/air filter modifications.

LOW-SPEED (PILOT) JET

The low-speed (pilot) jet controls fuel flow at one-eighth to one-fourth throttle. The low-speed (pilot) jet is usually not affected by most simple pipe/air filter modifications. However, a slightly lean low-speed (pilot) jet can cause havoc in the winter when its fuel is needed to help start the engine. You may find going one level up on this jet will help a winter cold start situation.

Finally, your idle mixture is revisited if you have a deceleration backfire situation. When you chop the throttle and use the motor to decelerate, if you get a stream of backfires you should try increasing your idle mixture strength one-fourth a turn at a time until the backfire goes away. (Note: If you reach a point where your idle mixture is four turns out [for fuel-type screws, NOT air-type screws], try going up one size on the slow-speed pilot jet and reset your idle mixture screw to one and a half turns out and repeat the process.)

If you have a soft hesitation, without a hard stumble, anywhere between one-fourth and three-fourths throttle, chances are your needle is lean, so raise the needle by lowering the clip. Conversely, if you have a hard stumble, chances are the needle position is rich, so lower the needle by raising the clip.

BUILDING AN ULTIMATE MUD MACHINE
DON'T GET BOGGED DOWN IN THE BIG ONES

Chapter 9

HERE WE WILL COVER

- Lift kits
- Monster mud tires
- More horsepower
- Snorkel kits
- Waterproofing techniques
- Getting the gunk out
- Winches
- Getting unstuck
- Mud riding tips

In real deep water crossings, if you feel the quad start to sink in the front, sit back on the seat to keep the air intake snorkel above the water line, stay on the throttle, and hope you meet solid ground real soon.

After installing oversized tires, retuning can regain lost power and also increase power to deliver the ATV's maximum performance.

There's a group of ATV riders who enjoy nothing better than testing the limits of their machines in mud and water. Some of these riders search out mud holes, while others don't have much of choice since they ride in a part of the country where the trails primarily run through the swamps. To keep from getting stuck every weekend, these riders have to perform some modifications to their vehicles to make them mud worthy.

Some will go all out in this effort, making specialized monster mud quads that can tackle unbelievable mud bogs. Keep in mind, however, that some of these mud monster quads lose some of their trail capabilities since they tend to have a much higher center of gravity, as well as having a rougher ride on dry ground with their big, heavy mud tires.

LIFT KITS

One of the most common ways of getting an ATV stuck in the mud is when the bottom of the machine "high-centers" on the mud after the tires dig in. To avoid this, your quad will need extra

ground clearance, and an ATV lift kit is the perfect solution. Bolt-on suspension modification is a relatively low-tech component and basically consists of a series of sturdy brackets.

The amount of clearance a kit provides is measured not from the body (body lift) but from the lowest point of ground contact. This in turn allows riders to go through deeper mud or water and over higher obstacles without becoming high-centered. It also gives them more options to install taller tires.

MUD TIRES

Mud tires are much larger and more aggressive than stock ATV tires. Stock tires are designed to be lightweight, have lower gross vehicle weight from the factory, and aren't necessarily designed for "real world" applications for extreme mud riders. More aggressive, higher ply, larger diameter tires allow riders to tackle more obstacles with their machines.

The disadvantages of adding larger, heavier tires is that they put more stress on the mechanics of the machine and increase the

wear-time of certain components, such as axles, drivetrains, transmissions, and engines.

So how big should you go with mud tires? Well, that depends on the size of your ATV's engine. Newer big-bores, such as the Brute Force, Grizzly, and Polaris 800s, for example, can handle tires up to the 29.5-inch High Lifter Outlaw. The lower cubic centimeter "big quads" (500cc to 600cc) can handle tires in the 25-inch to 28-inch range. In most cases, aftermarket wheels are required to allow for oversized tires.

Bigger tires do affect gearing of the ATV, just like in trucks. However, clutch kits and other modifications are available to make up for these additions.

When looking for the right mud tire, figure out what kind of rider you are. If you are a light mud rider, meaning you don't ride in mud all the time and spend time on trails and hard pack, you can purchase a less aggressive mud tire. The Outlaw MST would be a good choice. If you are aggressive in your riding, so your tire should be, too. Look for a six-ply tire for the most durability, deep lugs, sidewall wrap (to grip the ruts), and a flat profile to allow for a

smoother ride. Also, the lugs should feature "self-cleaning" properties, such as hollow sipes (cutaways in a tire's tread that allow for traction and grip) and curved lugs to allow for mud to be easily removed while riding.

MORE HORSEPOWER

Bigger, heavier tires require more horsepower to pull, and when you're dealing with mud machines, you're going to need all the ponies you can get. Virtually all riders who add big mud tires to their machines perform some sort of engine modification to regain some of the power lost by the addition of the tires.

These mods can include adding a performance exhaust, jet kit, or a better-breathing air filter. After installing oversized tires, retuning can regain lost power and also increase power to deliver the ATV's maximum performance. A clutch kit that is designed to improve low-end torque, improve shifting, and reduce belt slippage is the best answer to this problem.

Another way to gain back some horses is with a product called Power Now from High-Lifter. Power Now is a carburetor

Mud festivals and jamborees are big deals these days with hundreds of riders showing up for the fun in the muck. Check out www.highlifter.com for information on some of the big mud events in the South.

TIP

MUD TIRE PRESSURES

Do not run excessively low air pressure in your ATV's tires. Too low of an air pressure (three pounds or less) can cause the bead on the tire to become unseated and flatten the tire. It will then be much more difficult to fix in the field. A good range is between five to seven pounds. Also, for severe mud, use the higher air pressure, since doing that will make your tires a little taller and add some ground clearance.

How wacky do you want to be? Well, this mud monster ATV isn't just for show. It can actually navigate mud holes like no other vehicle can.

ALERT!

WATCH YOUR BRAKES

Mud riders will also want to pay particular attention to their brakes and wheel bearings. If you ride in water and mud that is axle deep, you should remove the tires and brake drums and clean out any accumulation of grit. If you don't, you will eventually ruin $200 worth of wheel bearings and brake pads before their time.

modification that allows more air to flow to the carb. This increases horsepower through engine efficiency due to uncompromised airflow velocity.

The ICM Module Power Pak is an ignition control module (black box) that is also available from High-Lifter. This modification remaps the factory spark advance, allowing the engine to reach its full potential all the way through the power band. This module was designed for V-twin engines and actually delivers "wheelstanding" performance. It costs around $100 and is one of the best performance mods you can get for the bucks.

If that's not enough, serious mud riders can add high-compression pistons, piston/cam packages, big-bore kits, and even nitrous kits to their ATVs. As far as costs go, this depends on how extreme you would like to get. Jet kits go for around $50, air filters are

about the same, while clutch kits and pipes are $100 to $300 and nitrous kits run $700 to $1,000! Ya gotta pay to play!

SNORKEL KITS

Snorkels are those funny looking pipes that stick up out of serious mud machines. They allow the quads to work like virtual submarines, pulling in and expelling air like a diver. Basically, a fully snorkeled ATV has an intake snorkel attached to the air box, an exhaust snorkel, and a clutch housing (belt-drive) snorkel.

The bad news is that snorkels are very tricky and hard for the backyard mechanic to pull off. And the consequences when things go wrong can be very expensive. When snorkeling your ATV, you can bet on one thing for sure—it will leak! Chances are good that you won't get everything right the first time. That's the advantage to purchasing a

To gain ground clearance and to allow your quad to use oversized mud tires, many riders install a lift kit, which raises the ATV's chassis several inches.

HighLifter
PRODUCTS

ATV LIFT KIT

Get 2 more inches of ground clearance with ATV Lift Kit.

"We highly recommend the High Lifter Kits for anyone wanting the maximum amount of ground clearance on their 4x4."
- Dirt Wheels Magazine

- More tire and fender clearance
- Run BIG Monster tires with no rubbing
- Made of steel brackets - strong and sturdy enough to hold up ATV
- Zinc plated for rust resistance and custom appearance
- Easy installation - ALL BOLT-ON *No Cutting, Welding Or Drilling*
- Complete detailed installation instructions
- Trained, experienced technical support staff

ATV Lift Kits available for most 4x4 models.

TIP

ONE AT A TIME THROUGH THE TOUGH STUFF

When mudding, it's always a good idea to ride in groups of two or more. Being stuck in a pretty bad hole all alone is never fun. If you have a friend on the trail with you, there's always a way out. Also, go one-at-a-time through the bad spots. This way, if the first guy gets stuck, you've still got one quad with all four wheels on the ground. Or if one guy breaks down, you've got another ATV to go after spare parts.

However, if you are riding in a line and the rider in front of you gets stuck, a simple bump from behind as he hits the throttle will usually get him out!

ATV tires built specifically for mud provide the ultimate in traction. However, getting a flat in the mud is a real bummer. Tire sealants are a great way to avoid that scenario. Air Lock tire sealant is one of the best on the market. It won't rust your wheels or dry out in your tire. It also plugs larger holes than any other brand, even in the sidewall.

On some ATV models, mud gets caked on the radiator and is hard to clean, making the engine overheat. This rider has utilized a High-Lifter Triple-Flow radiator that has been remounted on the front rack.

---

kit. The research and development that goes into snorkel kits such as Bayou Snorkels and Triangle ATV (both available from High Lifter Products) is immeasurable. When a quad with no snorkel, or worse, a nonfunctional homemade version is sunk, it can be a very expensive repair bill as the engine can get its insides all twisted up.

WATERPROOFING

There are a few things you can do to make your quad more waterproof. Some riders use silicone to seal certain components that are susceptible to water damage, such as hoses, snorkel components, and electrical connections. However, there's no way to seal everything for certain. Another must for serious mud riders are disc brakes. Honda drum brakes catch and hold mud and water and will eventually go bad because of it.

Another way to help prevent water from getting into your electrical connections is to pull them apart and apply dielectric grease into the fittings and then wrap them up good and tight with electrical tape.

Basically, the guy who does the most to protect his quad spends the least in repairing his quad. ATVs that are put through the rigors of mud riding are more likely to have repair issues than other users. The more preventative maintenance you perform on your quad—from oil changes to spark plug maintenance to regular cleaning—the more likely the ATV is to last.

GETTING THE GUNK OUT

Be careful when cleaning your ATV after a mud ride! Some guys and gals get home and pull out the pressure washer and blast everything off. Bad idea! Pressure washers can be too powerful for an ATV. They can tear hoses, break seals, and even crack plastic.

Take your time when you're cleaning your ATV after a ride and only use water with a pressure no greater than a garden hose with a nozzle. It can take a long time to get the job done right, but that's the price you pay for a good mud ride. You do want to hand clean your four-wheeler as soon as you can, though. The longer you wait, the more time the mud has to set, get hard, and do irreparable damage

You can break a few "safe riding" rules during a mud bog competition to keep the quad balanced and grabbing traction. If your ATV gets stuck with one wheel spinning wildly in the air and one on the ground not getting any traction at all, try tapping the front brake. This will often be enough to activate the positive traction feature of your front axle and transfer power to the wheel with more traction.

Serious mud boggers utilize snorkel-air intakes for the air box, exhaust, and transmission. High-Lifter Products sells some snorkel kits for specific models, but many snorkels are home-built. However, a word of caution since a leak can cause some catastrophic damage to your machine. This particular rider is running a dual exhaust setup, hence the two snorkels in the rear.

In competition mud bogs, you are likely to see riders leaning this way and that, trying to keep the quad balanced and grabbing traction.

to your engine and frame in the form of rust! To keep your wheels shining, use a product like Mirror Coat Metal Polish.

WINCHES

One of the most important accessories for mud riders is a winch. Virtually every serious mud bogger has a big ol' winch stuck on the front or the rear of his or her quad. Winches are good for you as well as your buddies. ATVs get stuck in the mud more than

anywhere else, so get at least a 2,500-pound winch if you're a serious mud addict. That size winch will handle most good-sized wheelers.

However, keep in mind that you're pulling more weight than just the weight of the ATV—the mud that's holding the quad accounts for weight as well. The ATV may only weigh 600 pounds, but the force at which mud holds the quad in place may triple or even quadruple that. That's why I recommend a bigger winch!

FRONT OR REAR MOUNT?

Most winches can either be mounted on the front or the rear of the ATV. There's really no advantage or disadvantage to the location. It just depends on how you're stuck. If your winch is on the front, you'll have to winch your four-wheeler through the hole that you're already in. If you mount it on the rear, you'll have to go backwards to get out. Ultimately, these are the questions to consider in this situation: Do I want to back up and try this hole again? Or do I want to winch forward and get out with the help of the winch to get past the hard stuff?

From my experience, about 80 percent of all winches are mounted on the front of the ATV and that's what I would suggest. There is, however, a winch accessory from Warn Industries called a multi-mount that will allow you to change from front to rear. It is a mounting kit that is connected to a receiver

Backyard mechanics go to just about any length when it comes to building mud bogging quads. These beefy front shocks appear to be off of a Jeep!

MUD-RIDING MECHANICS
GETTING THROUGH TO THE OTHER SIDE

The four basic keys to crossing a giant mud bog are momentum, traction, horsepower, and ground clearance.

In the case of momentum, it's best to follow in the ruts of the other riders who have already made it through the mud hole. You're always more likely to get stuck in "virgin mud."

However, at some point the path does get worse with use and the "line" gets rutted out. The bigger the quads are on the ride, the deeper the holes and ruts will get. One thing that can help you in these rutted situations is spacers. Spacers will increase the width of your quad by spacing the wheels out further. This allows your tires to grip the sides of ruts (increasing your traction) and keep turning. It is also possible to straddle ruts and ride across, but that gets tricky as ruts can be slippery and steep. However, to most mud riders, that's part of the fun of the ride.

Experienced riders can pick the best lines and spot the nastiest holes. Be comfortable and know the restrictions of your quad. For example, a Honda 300 4x4 will not go through the same holes as a Polaris 800 with 21 inches of ground clearance. It won't happen! So, if you ride a smaller quad, know what you can and cannot handle. Be willing to "sit a hole out," unless you like the challenge of getting stuck!

Body position, another piece of momentum, is a major factor in getting through a big mud hole. Keeping the quad balanced can only be achieved by shifting body weight. In competition mud bogs, you are likely to see riders leaning this way and that, laying across racks with one foot on the front rack, or both hands on one handlebar. All are in the effort to get the angle a rider needs to keep the quad balanced and grabbing traction.

In real deep water crossings, if you feel the quad start to sink in the front, sit back on the seat to keep the air intake snorkel above the water line, stay on the throttle, and hope you meet solid ground real soon.

If your ATV gets stuck with one wheel spinning wildly in the air and one on the ground not getting any traction at all, try tapping the front brake. This will often be enough to activate the positive traction feature of your front axle and transfer power to the wheel with more traction.

You'll also want to keep your speed down. Many riders have a tendency to hit the hole with a lot of throttle. All this does is spin the tires and dig holes. Remember the finesse rule. Keep your wheels turning slowly. Don't hit the gas abruptly; you'll only sink and get stuck.

Low gears are best for mud. Rocking back and forth keeps the tires touching the bottom in tough water/mud. If your tires aren't touching, you're spinning mud and that's not a good thing. (Although the roost makes for great pictures!) Some riders will want to get off the quad and push when things start looking tough. Be careful, though. Nothing is more painful, or embarrassing, than getting caught under an ATV in the mud. This is not a scuba sport!

Before riding in mud and/or water, grease every moving part you can. One of the best lubes to use is mining-grade industrial grease; it's real sticky and gooey and won't wash out. Something that might be easier to find is boat trailer wheel-bearing grease, which also resists water and mud. Clean and take apart nearly every moving component and bearing more often than you would if you were riding in dry conditions.

MUD-RIDING TECHNIQUES
LITTLE TRICKS TO MAKE A BETTER MUDDER

• Riding in lots of water could cause your foot brake pedal to eventually rust. Soak the shaft in penetrating oil to help keep it from rusting and freezing up.

• When towing a friend out of the mud, be sure to attach your tow strap (never use chains) at a low point on the quad that is about the same height as the axle. That gives you the best drive when pulling another quad.

• Before riding in mud and/or water, grease every moving part you can. One of the best lubes to use is mining-grade industrial grease; it's real sticky and gooey and won't wash out. Something that might be easier to find is boat trailer wheel-bearing grease, which also resists water and mud. Clean and take apart nearly every moving component and bearing more often than you would if you were riding in dry conditions.

• If your machine starts sputtering and missing while crossing streams, then you probably need to either get a new waterproof spark plug cap or apply dielectric grease to the spark plug boot. You should be able to find the grease in any auto parts store.

• Many of the top cross-country racers use a Twin-Air filter with Liquid Power Filter Oil (also available from Twin-Air). They claim it works great at keeping everything out of the air intake. If you want to simply waterproof your stock filter, add an Outerwears filter cover.

• To prevent damaging your ATV's front bumper and front racks when pushing buddies out of the mud, consider cutting up a heater hose and attaching it to the front end. That will prevent contact from scratching either machine.

• Be careful not to use power washers on your oil cooler or radiator fins. The high water pressure can flatten the tiny fins on your cooler or radiator decreasing flow and cooling efficiency.

• When winching another rider out of the mud, do not pull out some cable, hook it up, and then back up suddenly. Winches are designed to work best with a slow steady pull, not a sharp, jerking impact.

• Oversized tires suck up horsepower. Make sure you really need them before making the swap.

• One way to keep mud from building up on your quad is to spray a lubricant under the fenders and frame before the ride.

• Unless your quad runs strictly on dry surfaces, don't use an air box with holes in it or with the lid off! Aftermarket air boxes aren't good for deep water, either. You can make your stock setup even more waterproof by building a duct-tape guard around the air-scoop intake area to keep water from splashing in on the really wet rides.

• Anywhere there's wire penetration into the cases, seal it off with silicone. If there's a rubber boot at the base of it, secure it with a small zip-tie. Zip-ties can also be used on the rubber boots on the handlebar controls to keep mud out.

• Make sure the stator stays dry by checking to make sure the gasket is in good shape, and then seal off the cover with silicone.

• If your quad has sealed drum brakes, take them apart on a regular basis and wash the brake drum cover with water and detergent. This will make the brakes last quite a bit longer.

• If you spend a lot of time in deep water, you can re-route and add length to some of the vent tubes. However, don't get the overflow vent hose higher than the carb or it will flood the motor.

• When the differential gets hot and then cools during a long, deep stream crossing, the cooling air sucks water into the unit through the vent hose (if there is one). The same thing can happen with a crankcase vent hose. You can avoid this problem simply by installing a one-way check valve (make sure it's installed in the right direction!).

• Check all fluids (crankcase, tranny, shaft, front four-wheel drive) after a deep water ride to see if any of the oil is milky (a sure sign that water got in there). It's too late if you wait until you hear funny noises coming from the drivetrain—those types of repairs can be real expensive! If there is milky oil in the crankcase, you can still ride it to get home, but take it slow and easy. Change it as soon as you can, and then run it for a while. If it's still milky, change it again.

---

hitch. If you need the winch in the front, put it there. If you need it in the rear, pull the pin and move it to the back.

GETTING UNSTUCK

When using a winch, attach it to a tree or log but don't use another ATV as your anchor point unless it's your only choice. A four-wheeler that is really stuck will only pull the other ATV into the hole. If you tie off to a tree, you should always use a tree protector since winching damage can expose trees to disease and bugs.

Some riders carry a pulley system in their storage compartments or dry boxes.

Pulley systems are usually homemade, but some can be bought commercially. Pulleys can be attached to trees and then used in conjunction with the ATV's winch. This is a system that incorporates a large strap that wraps around a tree and connects using D-rings or hooks. The strap protects the tree from damage from the winch cable. Using this tree-hugger system and a pulley does two things: It protects the environment and it cuts in half the amount of weight being pulled by the winch. (Ain't physics a beautiful thing?)

Believe it or not, a weird way of getting your ATV unstuck is to use cat litter! Cat litter, poured on a mud hole, will harden the

mud around the quad, and a few minutes later, the ATV will crawl right out. Sounds crazy, but give it a try. A more conventional way of getting unstuck is to stack wood under the tires, provided you can find logs. This helps get the tires up out of the mud.

WHAT HAPPENS WHEN YOU HAVE A DROWN OUT?

Mud riders inevitably drown out their ATVs now and then. Whether it's just a matter of a little water splashing into the air box or a complete wipeout with water getting into the transmission, cylinder, etc., there is a step-by-step method to get back up and running out in the field (see Chapter 13 for the complete details of drown-out recovery).

ANECDOTE

CHECK FOR TROUBLES *BEFORE* THEY GET BIGGER!

One of the best ways to avoid serious mechanical problems with mud machines is to give your ATV a good once over after a good cleaning. I was recently working on my quad, and while looking it over I noticed that the brake line going to my front left brake was getting awful close to being pinched by some components at severe angles. If it were to get crimped, I would lose brake fluid on a ride and no brake fluid means no brakes. So I moved things around a bit to make sure the brake line was away from the trouble spot.

If you ride in the mud and put your quad away dirty, you'll never know what may be a problem in the future. It's easier and much cheaper to catch problems like that early.

The four basic keys to crossing a giant mud bog are momentum, traction, horsepower, and ground clearance. However, you don't want to get too crazy with the throttle. Many riders have a tendency to hit the hole with a lot of throttle and all this does is spin the tires and dig holes. The key is to keep your wheels turning slowly. Don't hit the gas abruptly; you'll only sink and get stuck.

ADVANCED TRAIL RIDING TECHNIQUES
TACKLING THE TERRAIN LIKE A PRO

Chapter 10

Freestyle tricks like these are for expert riders only! These guys were top-flight jumpers and racers well before they ever started taking a hand off the bars or hiking a leg over the seat.

A misconception among the general public is that riding ATVs doesn't take very much effort or skill. In a way, that's true if all you're doing is cruising along on a flat, smooth, wide gravel path on an old railroad bed. However, very few of us confine ourselves to that type of casual riding.

To go fast on a tough and challenging trail with rocks, ruts, bumps, jumps, hillclimbs, off-cambers, and lots of turns takes loads of skill and will give any rider a good physical workout. Admittedly, many of the riding techniques used to smoothly and quickly navigate difficult trails eventually come to most riders after years of experience. To get a head start on advanced trail riding techniques, though, and to avoid picking up any bad habits, this chapter will detail the essential things you'll need to know to tackle the terrain like a pro.

ATTACK STANCE

The attack stance for riding ATVs allows riders to be ready for anything on the trail. This dynamic position is almost identical to the attack stance expert dirt bike riders use.

Basically, the attack stance is when the rider is standing in a crouched position with knees and elbows bent, head looking up and forward, with the rider's weight centered over the footpegs. The rider's elbows are out to the side (not in or up) and his or her arms and legs are bent at roughly 90-degree angles.

While in the attack stance, riders are able to quickly move their weight forward, sideways, or rearwards—depending on what's ahead on the trail. In addition, with their arms and legs bent, riders are able to quickly absorb the shocks of any bumps or jars to the machine. And when something unexpected pops up such as an obstacle, they'll be much more able to quickly turn, stop, or gas it than they would if they were sitting on the seat in a static position. You may also want to keep a finger or two on the front brake in this stance. And if your quad has a manual clutch, keep a finger or two on the clutch lever as well. This way you're ready to grab either lever in a fraction of a second if need be.

Some jumps, like the double jump pictured here, require the rider to get enough height and distance to clear the second jump. On other kinds of jumps, the rider may want to decrease airtime to get the driving rear wheels back down on the ground as soon as possible.

While in the attack stance, riders are able to quickly move their weight forward, sideways, or rearwards—depending on what's ahead on the trail.

Wheelies are one of the most fun things you can do on a sport or high-performance ATV. After a little practice, you can find the "balance point" and ride a wheelie indefintely.

The variations of the attack stance depend on whether you're on level ground or climbing or descending a hill. On level ground, your weight will be centered over the footpegs and the middle of the seat, while hillclimbs require your attack stance to move forward with your chin past the handlebars and your head looking up and forward. On tough, fast downhills, your attack stance will be centered over the back of the machine with your arms and legs outstretched, yet still slightly bent to absorb shocks.

With the exception of fast, smooth straightaways, most cross-country and motocross (MX) racers spend the majority of their track time in the attack stance. Very aggressive and fast trail riders do so as well, with the limiting factor being their own physical stamina! It takes a lot more strength and endurance than one might think to ride a bucking quad for any length of time in the attack stance, and top ATV racers need to be as fit as any other high-level athlete. (To get better endurance by "riding light," see the accompanying sidebar in this chapter.)

TURNS AND CORNERING

Going around corners in an aggressive, fast manner is one of the most fun things you can do on an ATV. Backing it in like a sprint car driver, spinning the rear end around, and shooting out of the corner with the front wheels clawing in the air is one of the reasons we go to so much effort to partake in this sport.

This classic cornering shot shows the rider hanging his weight to the inside, front wheels turned in the opposite direction to control the spinout with the rider hard on the gas as he races to the next corner.

This rider has just completed the corner and has set his weight back on the seat for maximum traction. The front wheels lofting into the air can attest to that.

RIDE LITE
GO FASTER AND CUT DOWN ON FATIGUE

Probably more than anything, "riding light" is something that separates the top racers from all the rest. By not fighting their quad through the rough stuff, they are able to save their energy and avoid the dreaded "arm pump" and overall fatigue. Also by riding light, their ATV will be smoothly skimming over the obstacles, rather than slamming and bucking like a bronco. The top racers who ride light have a jumping style that seems effortless. Their landings are smooth and soft compared to the backmarkers.

OK, so how do they perform these magical feats? Riding light is actually more of a mental game than a physical one. Most of it comes from lots of experience and practice. Basically, you become "one with the quad" by anticipating how it will react to obstacles and throttle input. Being one step ahead of your machine gives you the opportunity to prepare for anything ahead of time, thereby saving you from fighting the ATV.

All this results in a lot less effort on your part, and therefore less fatigue at the end of the trail ride or race. When everything is clicking just right, you'll feel like your feet are floating on the footpegs and the handlebars are as easy to turn as a kiddy's tricycle.

You can work on riding light by concentrating on loosening your grip on the bars and moving more "catlike" when you shift your weight back and forth on your quad. Once you have the feeling, you'll know what we're talking about and it will probably become an important part of your riding skills.

Steep hills are one of the trickiest maneuvers you'll ever do on an ATV. Pick a good line, hit the throttle, keep your momentum up, and put your weight far forward, and you'll soon find yourself topping some nasty inclines.

There are basically two types of corners on the trail: tight corners and longer radius corners called sweepers. Each has a different technique for going fast, and even that can vary depending on the roughness of the trail and the type of trail surface (gravel, sand, loam, hardpack, etc.). However, there are some good basic guidelines you can follow.

TIGHT TURNS

For tight corners, come in hot (fast) in the attack stance and brake hard at the last minute with both the front and rear brakes. Just as you're entering the turn, release the front brake, move your body forward and to the inside of the turn, weighting the inside footpeg. At the same time, turn your handlebars and jam on the rear brake, locking up your rear tires.

If you're riding a sport or high-performance ATV with a manual clutch, pull the clutch in and rev the engine as you're doing your first braking for the corner. Downshift to the gear you want to come out of the corner in, which is usually second or third gear.

The rear braking action will pivot the rear of your four-wheeler around the tight corner. If you need to continue the "spin-out" to complete the corner, dump the clutch

You have to slow down for a big log crossing. The trick is to blip the throttle just before impact, and then get your weight back as the rear suspension soaks up the hit. Be careful that you don't get booted in the rear end by the seat or the racks!

and gas it—the spinning rear tires will continue the slide. As you exit the corner, move your weight back on the seat and get back on full throttle as soon as you're pointed in the right direction.

SWEEPING CORNERS

If you've ever watched dirt sprint cars back it into a corner, you'll get a good idea of how to broadside an ATV. Come into the corner fast and initiate the slide by putting your weight to the inside and turning the handlebars. If your front end is not getting enough traction, it will "push" through the corner without turning. Solve that problem by putting your weight more forward to lighten the rear end and get more traction in the front. You can also grab just a tad of front brake to get the quad turning on slippery surfaces such as gravel. Another way to get the rear end sliding is to jab at the rear brake.

Once you're sliding, the real fun begins! You control the slide with two things: the handlebars and the throttle. Once the quad is sideways, turn the bars the opposite way to keep it in a controlled slide. The more throttle you give it, the more the rear wheels will spin and the farther around it will slide. If it feels like you're going to spin out, let off on the throttle a bit and the rear tires will get more traction and straighten you out. Be careful though; if you let off too abruptly (chopping the throttle), the outside tires might catch and send you into a "highside" flip.

As the turn ends, get your weight back up on the seat of the quad to get more traction

Blasting through big whoops is one of the most tiring things you can do on a quad. The big, smooth bumps naturally form on the sandy soils of racetracks and trails and require precise throttle control and body positioning. Note how the riders are in the "attack stance."

to the rear end, which will straighten you out. You may also have to let off the throttle for a fraction of a second to stop the rear tires from spinning. From there, you just tuck down and gas it to the next corner.

JUMPING

There are a handful of things that help cushion the landing when jumping a quad: two front shocks, one or two rear shocks, two arms, and two legs. One thing that doesn't work is your butt on the seat! Sitting down on takeoff or landing will hurt at the very least, and might buck you right off at the worst.

There are three things you can do as you hit the face of the jump:

A) *keep a steady throttle,*
B) *Let off on the throttle,*
C) *Or blip the throttle.*

Each one will do something different with the quad once you're in the air. Which one you use depends on how far you want to fly off the jump and whether you want to land rear wheels first or front wheels first.

Going off a jump with a steady throttle will get you big air and lots of distance. At the races, you'll see the motocross guys hitting double and triple jumps with lots of speed and throttle. However, on the trail you'll probably be using the "blip the throttle" method more often. By approaching a trail jump with a low or medium throttle setting and then gassing it for a fraction of a second just as you hit the face of the jump, you'll be doing things such as compressing the suspension to get a little "hop" in the air as you leave the jump and

Rock fields have to be navigated slowly and carefully. Let the quad move underneath you and make adjustments with your body weight to keep it balanced.

Surprisingly, one of the keys to going fast on the track or trail is having excellent braking skills. The later and harder you can hit the brakes before a corner, the faster you'll be going. Hit both the front and rear brakes hard just before the corner while you're still going straight, keeping your weight centered over the quad in a standing position.

Traversing a rocky downhill section can be scary on just about any off-road vehicle. On an ATV, the main thing to concentrate on is keeping it slow and not allowing a front wheel to get stuck in a hole.

As far as body language goes when jumping, always approach the jump in the attack stance. As you hit the face of the jump, keep your upper body forward with your arms and legs bent and chin up. As the quad takes off, let it rise up underneath you slightly at the highest point of the jump, and then push the handlebars and pegs down, straightening your legs slightly.

With your arms and legs extended, you'll have more "suspension travel" in your body as the quad lands. Your arms and legs should act just like the shock absorbers on your quad as you hit the ground. Then you quickly raise your body back up into the attack stance, all ready for the next obstacle.

Common mistakes made while jumping include hitting the throttle too hard on takeoff, which will put your quad into a big wheelie in the air. Another mistake jumpers make is letting off the throttle too much on takeoff, which puts your ATV into a dangerous nosedive. You can sometimes save that situation by hitting the throttle in the air (the spinning rear wheels will start to bring the front end up), but don't count on it. When it comes to jumping quads, start off on small easy jumps to get a feel for what can happen, before graduating to more difficult leaps.

BIG BUMPS AND WHOOPS

Big bumps and whoops are basically the same thing. They are generally found on racetracks, but commonly form naturally on sandy trails. They are a lot of fun for most riders and really give you a good workout.

The key to jamming through the whoops is to keep your weight to the back of the quad (in the attack stance, of course) and keep the front wheels high and skimming on the tops of the bumps. Depending upon the spacing of the whoops, you'll want to keep a steady throttle in a strong gear range. Some whoops can be hopped over and jumped by using a varying throttle.

When you're hitting whoops fast, the quad will be rocking back and forth and you'll be flexing your arms and legs in a smooth and fluid motion, always returning to the attack stance.

There are several ways of getting in trouble in the whoops. One is when you let the front wheels drop into the bottom of the trough. When that happens, hang on tight and try to keep the wheels pointed straight and hope for the best. Another common problem when tackling the whoops at high speed is having the rear shock "packup." This

you'll be getting the front end in the air so you land rear wheels first, which is preferable off most jumps.

Letting off, or "chopping," the throttle on takeoff decreases the amount of air you get and causes your quad to nosedive and land front wheels first. You may want to use that technique off a peaked uphill jump where the landing is on a steep downslope. That can also work on a road crossing or "tabletop" jump.

happens because the whoops are being hit so fast that the shock doesn't have time to extend for the next hit, and in effect they hit the next whoop compressed and don't do their job. That means you'll get booted in the butt by your seat and might be knocked out of control. The solution is to either slow down or buy a high-performance racing shock for your quad.

HILLCLIMBS

Let's get something straight right off the bat here: Hillclimbs have probably wrecked more quads than any other trail obstacle out there. If you don't make it up a steep, nasty hill, your quad may very well end up in a heap at the bottom and you'll be lucky to not have it land on you. With that in mind, if you always stick to hills that you know, you have a very good chance of topping safely, and you'll have a much more enjoyable (and longer lived!) ATV riding career.

OK, so what's the trick to hillclimbing? Three things: momentum, traction, and line selection. Start your hilltopping quest by carefully looking at your lines (options). Choose the one that appears to have the least amount of obstacles and the best traction. Charge up the hill in the attack stance with the most speed you can safely carry from the bottom (momentum). As soon as you hit the face of the hill, get your weight as far forward as possible to keep the front end down and stay on the gas. Keep the engine in a gear that keeps the rear wheels driving. Don't let the engine revs bog down or you'll be in trouble. If you have a manual-shifting machine, you may have to downshift, but do it quickly!

Keep the front end planted enough to be able to steer and try to stick to your chosen line. Stay on it and you'll top the hill. If things go wrong and you aren't going to make it, you've got two choices—either try to quickly turn around with your remaining momentum,

Steep dropoffs can be navigated with quads as long as you have your weight as far back as possible and keep your momentum going downhill. A sudden stop at this point in the maneuver could send the quad into a nosedive and rollover.

ALERT!

WHEN IN DOUBT, GAS IT!

One of the weirdest things you'll ever hear about off-road riding is the old dirt bike adage "when in doubt, gas it!" The deal is, it's true, and it works for ATVs, too.

Say you're blazing down the trail at a pretty good clip and you suddenly see a big washout rut right across the trail. No matter what, you aren't going to be able to completely stop in time. The thing to do in this situation is to let off the throttle, jam on both brakes hard, and try to stop. When you see you aren't going to make it, let off the brakes, get your weight back, and hit the throttle right before you hit. This will get the front end light, and allow your rear wheels to hit the opposite side of the rut.

With your weight already back, you're better prepared for the impact. If you hit the rut with your brakes locked up, the front end will drop in and you'll probably be pitched over the front. This same procedure should work for other obstacles that suddenly pop up, such as logs, rocks, and bumps. If you're really going fast, you may only have enough time to get your weight back and gas it without doing any braking.

Even sport/utility quads can be good sliders in the right conditions. Basically, you turn the bars, weight the inside peg, crank on the gas to get the rear wheels spinning, and then turn the bars into the direction of the skid.

HOW TO BAIL
YOU DON'T WANT IT TO HAPPEN . . . BUT IF IT DOES, DO IT RIGHT

Fortunately, most ATV riders never experience a hard crash. However, as your riding skills increase, so does your speed and that means when something goes wrong it's going to be more serious. You may think that once a crash begins there's not much you can do. Experienced riders will argue otherwise, as many of them know a few tricks that may lessen your chances of getting hurt.

The most obvious way to protect you in the event of a wreck is to wear all the necessary protective gear (see Chapter 2). If you're riding in rocky areas or in the desert (yucca plants and cactus, oh my!), you may want to opt for the extra protection of a chest protector.

The key to avoiding injury in an ATV crash is to get away from the vehicle. A typical highside in a corner, where the tires suddenly catch in the middle of slide, basically sends you flying on your own. As soon as it's obvious that the quad is going to tip and there's no saving it, let go of the bars and prepare for the launch. Once you

hit the ground, the trick is to tuck and roll. It's the same maneuver football players, snow skiers, and other outdoor athletes use when they're knocked down. The one thing you don't want to do is "stiff arm" into the ground. Continue to tuck and roll as your speed dissipates.

One of the most dangerous crashes is "looping out," or wheelying back, on a hillclimb. As you're heading off the quad, kick away from it as much as possible before it comes back and hits you. If you do see it coming, draw your legs into chest to protect your head and upper body.

An endo-type spill (nosediving and flipping forward) is a rare, but dangerous type of crash. There's not much you can do in that type of crash, but if it's at all possible throw yourself to the side as you're being bucked off because that ATV is going to be slamming down right behind you.

Of course, your best bet for not getting hurt in a crash is not riding over your head and getting in trouble in the first place!

This rider is landing from a very high jump and you can see how both the machine's suspension and the rider's body is soaking up the landing. Notice too how the rider stays in the "attack position."

On some jumps such as tabletops and double jumps where the landings are a downslope, the perfect landing is with the nose of the quad slightly down. If you feel the front end of the quad dropping too much, hit the throttle to raise it back up (this works even when you're airborne).

being careful to keep your weight uphill, or simply stop your quad and regroup. Don't try rolling backwards down the hill!

DOWNHILLS

Going down steep hills on an ATV is much easier than going up! Basically, you'll want to put your weight way over the back end to keep the front wheels as light as possible. Use engine braking by shifting down (or with an automatic, engaging low range) to help keep the speed reasonable. If you're still going too fast, use both brakes just to the point of locking up the tires. Even on the steepest hills, by using these methods you should be able to crawl down the hill if need be.

To go fast, simply stay loose and move with the machine as it careens downhill, but be prepared to get on the binders if things start getting out of control. Remember while braking that a locked-up front wheel won't turn and locked-up rear wheels slither around sideways.

OBSTACLES

The main key to going fast over ledges, ruts, logs, and holes is to keep your front end light and blip the throttle. Let the rear suspension soak up the majority of the hit. Do this by approaching the obstacle in the attack stance and easing off the throttle. Right before you hit the obstacle with your front wheels, pull

Finding yourself 10 feet in the air with the front end of your quad too high is not something to strive for. If you can think fast enough to tap the rear brake, that could help (the gyroscopic effect of stopping the spinning rear wheels drops the front end down). You could avoid the scenario in the first place by chopping the throttle right before takeoff for that particular jump.

Tackling tight, twisty wooded trails is all about confidence, rhythm, and finesse. You gain a lot of technique simply by experience.

back on the bars, get your weight to the back, and blip the throttle, all at the same time. Your front end shouldn't have much of an impact, and if your two rear wheels hit the obstacle at the same time, the rear shock will take the hit just fine. However, be prepared for the rear end to kick up a bit, as the front end comes back down to the ground.

One of the mistakes with obstacles is hitting them too fast, which may kick the rear end up so high that it will knock you off. Another mistake is skidding into the obstacle with the brakes on. When that happens, the front suspension is compressed and just slams into the face of the obstacle rather than popping over it.

TIGHT WOODS

Tackling tight, twisty wooded trails is all about confidence, rhythm, and finesse. You gain a lot of technique simply by experience. You'll need to use a lot of body language to make the transition from turn to turn smoothly and quickly. The key to not hitting trees with your front wheels is to always be looking ahead and making precise turns between the trees. Going fast through the woods is no place to be going over the edge and getting out of shape. Just getting off line a little can be a painful experience.

SNOW, ICE, AND SAND

When riding on trails with snow, ice, or sand, you'll have to change your riding style to accommodate the change in traction. You may find that you'll have to move your weight more drastically to get traction to the front or rear of the machine. If you go into an icy corner and the quad doesn't want to turn, get your weight up over the handlebars

and push down to get some bite to the front tires. As soon as the corner is made, get your rear end plopped on the back of the seat to get maximum traction to the rear wheels. You'll be moving around a lot more than if you were on dirt, but it's certainly fun!

Top motocross racers keep at least one finger on the clutch and one on the front brake for most of the race, always on the ready for a quick engagement. Notice how this racer is already getting his body weight to the inside for the upcoming turn.

TIP

WHEELIES CAN BE YOUR FRIEND

We've all seen the guy in the parking lot who likes to do wheelies. Sure they're fun and they look cool, but they also have a practical use out on the trail. Say you need to get over a really big log or rock ledge. Do a quick wheelie to get your front end over. Say you come along a small stream or rut. Wheelie your way over it.

How do you do a wheelie, though? On an automatic four-wheeler, sit to the back of the seat, gas it, and pull up on the bars. With a manual shift, rev it up, pop the clutch, and pull back on the bars. To ride a wheelie, find the balance point by varying the throttle and tapping the rear brake. If you feel you're going to tip over backwards, tap the rear brake to settle the front end back down. If you do go too far, the grab bar should save you from completely going over backwards.

If you go into an icy corner and the quad doesn't want to turn, get your weight up over the handlebars and push down to get some bite to the front tires.

ATV COMPETITIONS
ALL ABOUT THE WONDERFUL WORLD OF RACING

Chapter 11

HERE WE WILL COVER

- **Motocross racing**
- **Cross-country racing**
- **TT/short track racing**
- **Desert/endurance racing**
- **Ice racing**
- **Hillclimbs**
- **Sand and dirt drags**
- **Riding to win**

Ice racing is one of the easiest forms of ATV competition as far as wear and tear on man and machine goes. The competition, however, is usually fast and furious as they duke it out with studded tires on the frozen lakes of the northern half of the country.

There has been at least one national ATV circuit running continuously since the early 1980s.

Just about anything with an engine eventually ends up being raced in this country. All-terrain vehicles are no exception and actually have a long racing history. There has been at least one national ATV circuit running continuously since the early 1980s. There are also a wide variety of types of competitions, although certain kinds of racing are regional in nature.

Nearly all forms of ATV racing are based on similar competitions in the motorcycle world. In fact, most local ATV racing is usually run in conjunction with the dirt bike programs. In this chapter, the most popular forms of ATV competitions in the country today are discussed, as well as tips on how to set up a quad for that type of racing.

MOTOCROSS

Motocross racing is the most popular type of ATV racing in the country, and therefore the easiest to find events to participate in. The tracks are characterized by lots of jumps with right and left turns and are usually fairly wide.

Nearly every heavily populated area in the country has a motocross track nearby. Some tracks are all man-made on a flat plot of land, while others also utilize natural terrain such as hills and valleys.

Motocross is also the most physically demanding of all the ATV disciplines. To win, you have be a great jumper and a hard charger in the turns. You must be able to handle whoops, braking bumps, and perhaps an uphill and downhill section.

Some may say it's a young man's sport, but there's usually several vet classes offered at the bigger events and a lot of those guys still haul. The key to going fast on an MX track is not so much being young as being in great physical shape. Motocross is primarily designed for sport and high-performance ATVs only.

The races typically last 10 to 15 minutes, and everyone races twice during the day against the same riders (called a moto). The overall winner is the one who has the lowest score after they add up your finishing orders for the day (for example, a 1-3 beats a 4-1). In the case of a tie, the rider who got the best score in the second moto wins. Sometimes riders can win the overall with a 2-3 or less when the race winners have rotten luck in their other moto.

To compete in the amateur motocross classes, there are some basic mods you'll have to make before your first race. For safety purposes, virtually every motocross track requires all ATVs to have a kill switch. This is a tether cord attached to the rider and the kill button on the handlebars. If the rider falls off, the engine stops and keeps the quad from continuing to run off the track. Another safety mod most motocrossers make before doing anything else is adding padded bars around the footpegs.

In the lower amateur classes, you can compete and have fun with no more modifications than perhaps a change of rear tires. But if you want to win in the top classes of motocross, there are more modifications you'll need to perform. Anything to make your engine faster (see Chapter 8) is a plus, especially in the important race to the first turn. Next, you'll want to improve the handling of your ATV by re-valving your rear shock or buying front and rear racing shocks. Many motocrossers also invest in a wider rear axle, bumpers, beadlock rims, different handlebars, clutch, etc. By perusing any one of the ATV magazines, you'll find that you can change virtually every part on your quad in your quest to make an ultimate (albeit expensive!) motocross racer.

CROSS COUNTRY

Close behind motocross in popularity is cross-country (XC) racing. Like motocross and TT, cross country has a national circuit as well as many regional events (typically referred to as hare scrambles, or simply scrambles), primarily located in Midwestern and eastern states. Like its name suggests, cross-country events take place on long, looped natural-terrain trails. XC racers typically encounter hillclimbs, stream crossings, rocks, dust, mud bogs, and, of course, twisty, wooded trails. Many of the national tracks also encompass a full-blown motocross track in the loop as well. Before the race, riders are not allowed to practice on the course, but can walk it if they want.

The races last around two to two and half hours and the riders take off in waves of the different classes. Each rider is carefully recorded by time at the end of each lap and at the checkers; riders are scored by their divisions, as well as being awarded an overall finishing order. Pit stops for fuel are common at XC events and many times flat tires have to be changed as well.

Cross-country racing is probably the easiest to prepare for as far as machine modifications go. You can virtually race

Long distance desert racing has its own special charm of man and machine against the elements. The ATVs used in this sport are modified for top-end power, longer travel suspension, and, most importantly, rugged reliability.

Flattrack, or TT racing, is probably the most primitive form of ATV competition, dating back to the very early days of three-wheelers. Riders sweep around a smooth dirt road course that typically features several rolling jumps.

TIP

WINNING THE RACE THE NIGHT BEFORE

The top racers are generally the ones who are the most prepared before they even get to the track. Don't wait until race morning to clean the air filter or change the handlebars. You never know how long the sign-up line is, or if you're dealing with weather problems on the way to the track.

WHERE TO RACE
HOW TO SEARCH FOR EVENTS

Unfortunately, there isn't one central source to turn to for all the ATV race schedules in the United States. However, there are some places to check that have a lot of info on racing action. First and foremost is the All-Terrain Vehicle Association (ATVA). This is a sister organization to the American Motorcyclist Association (AMA) and is the single biggest organizing body for ATV racing. The ATVA runs the three major ATV racing series in the country: the GNC (Grand National Championship) Motocross Series, the GNC TT Series, and the GNCC Cross Country Series. The majority of these events take place in the eastern half of the country, though several times a year they do venture west.

In addition to the major series, the ATVA sanctions local races in nearly every state and it publishes its schedules in a newsletter (combined, the AMA and ATVA sanction nearly 4,000 events a year!). To race at an ATVA-sanctioned event, you must first become a member of the organization (costs around $40 and you can usually sign up right at the track).

To contact the ATVA, check its website at www.ATVAonline.com or call (866)ATVA-JOIN.

To find out about non-ATVA events in your area, your best bet is to check with the local dealerships. They usually know what's going on in the area. Nearly every motocross track in the country has a quad class, as do almost all cross-country events. Also watch for posters and fliers at gas stations and cafes when traveling in your neck of the woods. And when the county fairs start popping up, carefully check their schedule of events for ATV competitions. The monthly ATV magazines and the many ATV websites are also a good source for info on upcoming races.

The top racers have usually perfected a way of choosing an alternate line on the track to get around a competitor. If you wait for the guy in front of you to make a mistake, you may be stuck behind him for the entire event.

This ATV takes the term "racing modifications" to the extreme. It was built for the Pikes Peak Hillclimb Exhibition class and features a large-bore street bike engine.

TIP

GET TO THE TRACK EARLY

Even if you're all packed up the night before with your machine fueled up and ready to go with the right tires and equipment, you should get to the track as early as possible. Many tracks let the riders choose their spot on the line for the first races in the order they signed up. And no matter how well-prepared you are, something always seems to pop up at the last minute at the races. Missing your practice session can be a real bummer, but fortunately many tracks have what they call a "late practice."

---

showroom stock machinery in the amateur classes and there are plenty of opportunities for riders with utility and sport/utility machines.

Like motocross, physical conditioning is a key to winning in the top classes, but riders can still be competitive in the lower divisions by riding at a less demanding pace (you can read that as meaning you don't have to train as hard!).

Serious cross-country riders will perform engine mods for more horsepower, but always with an eye for reliability rather than all-out speed. In fact, building "toughness" into a cross-country ATV is important as it can take quite a pounding during the event. Everything from tires, to skid plates, to air filter socks have reliability and protection from the elements in mind.

TT AND SHORT TRACK

This is probably the most primitive form of ATV racing. TT tracks are smooth and wide and feature only rolling bumps and jumps as compared to the much more rough and tumble world of motocross. They are laid out with right and left turns, like a car-racing road course. However, along with the tamer track layout come higher speeds. Early in most TT events, the track develops a "blue-groove," which is a line of rubber laid down from the soft compound tires. There is a ton of traction in this groove and the tires can actually be heard to squeal as the ATV slides through the corners.

Unlike motocross, TT events feature heat races and then a winner-take-all main

Some asphalt dragstrips have classes for ATVs, resulting in some really wild dragster quad creations. More common are ATV sand drag competitions that are popular in California, Oregon, Oklahoma, and Michigan.

Several female ATV riders have been competitive in some of the top classes with the guys. The ATVA National Motocross, TT, and Cross Country series all feature a women's class that gains a lot of attention with the fans every week.

First Place

TIP

FIGURING OUT THE CLASSES

Depending upon the type of event you're at, choosing a class to compete in can be a bit confusing. At the bigger races, there are a lot of classes offered, and some riders may be able to enter several different divisions with the same machine if they choose. Classes are generally divided by the engine size of the machine and the age (or gender) of the rider.

Some of the more popular classes have separate divisions within, usually called A, B, and C. The A class would be for the fastest, most experienced riders, while the B class is made of intermediates, and the C class is reserved for riders in their first year of racing. And some tracks simply use the words expert, intermediate, and beginner in their classifications. The pro and semi-pro classes have higher entry fees since a portion of their money is used for the purse.

---

event (the heats determine starting position for the finals). The length of the races is similar to motocross (10 to 15 minutes for the mains). TT racing is not as physically demanding as motocross, but riders can still get pretty whipped trying to hang on to these high-horsepower, high-traction machines.

The key to setting up a winning TT machine is to build a fast engine, get the proper gearing, lower the chassis (you do that by lowering the shock mounts or changing to shorter shocks), and putting on a set of big, soft compound slick tires. To have any success at TT, a beginning racer should at least have slicks, a sway bar, and a lowered chassis. Unfortunately, one of the biggest expenses for TT racers is the cost of the rear tires, which can wear out after only one or two events. Like

MX racing, you don't see any utility or sport/utility quads on the track.

Short-track ATV racing is like TT in virtually all aspects except that the tracks are small, left-turn-only ovals with no jumps. They can range in length from tiny speedway tracks (one-eighth to one-sixth of a mile) to full-blown, half-mile dirt, stock car tracks. Some riders use offset axles and bigger tires on the right side to help the quads stick in the corners. The thrills in short-track racing are extreme as some of the four-wheelers can run wide open all the way around on some of the bigger tracks.

DESERT AND ENDURANCE RACING

When you hear the words Baja 1000, what comes to mind? Yeah, that's right—cactus, snakes, rough and dusty trails, and grueling runs all through the night. Baja is certainly the most famous of those types of events, but there are a lot of other ones held in the far western states every year. Sometimes they are point-to-point races, while other times they are held on big loops. The courses are all natural terrain and get pretty chewed up since the ATVs are usually sharing the track with hundreds of dirt bikes, or in the case of Baja, the trucks and buggies.

Of course, the key to winning a desert endurance race is to first finish. Like the cross-country quads, desert racing machines are built to last. They generally sit taller than other ATV racers by installing long-travel shocks and wider A-arms. The seats are also replaced with higher versions so the transition from standing to sitting is lessened. Skid plates are very important, as well as tough tires and wheels and a larger fuel tank.

Perhaps what distinguishes desert racing the most from other forms of ATV competition is the added logistics of running such a long event. You'll have to set up pits at certain parts of the course to stop for more fuel and make any repairs. In the longer events like Baja, there are typically many rider changes during the race. Sometimes, the pit crews will have to perform major repairs, such as changing a swingarm or a piston, to make it to the finish.

One of the great things about cross-country racing is the fact that there is a class for just about every type of machine and rider skill level. Cross-country tests the riders skills on just about every type of terrain typically found on a trail ride— rocks, hills, mud, and lots of twisty woods sections.

Like the cross-country quads, desert racing machines are built to last.

Organized ATV hillclimb competitions are a rarity, but they do exist, mainly in the northeast and Mid-Atlantic states. They are always in conjunction with motorcycle hillclimbs. The wrecks are spectacular but usually injury-free for the rider. (The same can't be said the ATV!)

Recently, ATV endurance racing has made its way east. There are now several 12- and 24-hour events on much smaller (compared to Baja!) natural terrain and man-made tracks. Like cross-country racing, endurance events usually have classes for utility and sport/utility machines.

ICE RACING

Ice racing four-wheelers is a real hoot. It's probably one of the safest types of racing you can enter, as well as being the least tiring. The races are held on frozen lakes and the courses are most commonly a simple oval, or they can be patterned after a road course.

The format is similar to TT with heats and qualifiers and then a main event at the end of the day. The races themselves are quite short, usually less than 10 minutes each. Basically, the hot setups for an ice racing ATV are identical to that for TT except that the tires have small sheet metal screws (studs) stuck in for traction. The

number and style of the screws is an art form in itself, and riders are continually trying to find a better setup. In fact, different ice and weather conditions actually require different studding and tire tactics.

One of the easiest forms of ATV competitions to enter is the un-studded sport and utility classes at the ice races. Like the name implies, no studding is allowed but the competition is still hot!

HILLCLIMBS

Hillclimb competitions for ATVs are not very common, taking place primarily in the East Coast states. But they are spectacular to watch as the quads try to tackle the same short, steep hills that the dirt bikes ride on. Some of the hills even feature jumps on the way up.

ATV hillclimbers have many of the same modifications that a motocross quad has, except that they usually sport an extremely long swingarm. The longer wheelbase keeps them from wheeling over on the way up.

FIRST TURN JITTERS FOR BEGINNERS

Probably the most dangerous time for first-time racers is the start. Beginners are usually all pumped up for that first blast to the first turn and are determined to get a good start. However, a common mistake is that they get so excited that they come in too fast and blow through the corner, usually taking a couple of riders out with them.

The key to avoiding this is to practice several starts during the practice session and understand that the most important thing is to brake and make the corner! You'll have plenty of other races to get the hole shot. Settling for a mid-pack start is a much better way to start your racing career than causing a crash.

The format is pretty simple: Hillclimbers get two shots at the hill during the day, with their best climb counting as their final score. If they don't make it up, the distance is their score and if they top the hill, their time is the score.

If you've ever witnessed a hillclimbing quad that doesn't make it to the top and then tumbles all the way to the bottom, you might understand why this particular sport is not very popular. Fortunately, though, there's usually a hill crew stationed at the steep sections, armed with big hooks and ropes, which they use to snag the ATV before it flips to the bottom.

There's another type of ATV racing that is called hillclimbing, but it is quite different from what is described above. It's a western series that includes the famous Race to the Clouds, a.k.a. the Pikes Peak Hillclimb. Quads, usually in a TT setup, race up the twisty 12-mile gravel and asphalt road on the same day the cars and motorcycles run. Their times, in fact, are quite impressive and generally top some of the dirt bike classes.

Professional ATV racing has come a long way in the past couple years with big haulers and lots of sponsors. Work hard at the local level and you could garner a few sponsors yourself.

To set your quad up for TT racing, you'll need to lower the chassis, add a front swaybar, and, most importantly, bolt on some racing slicks. Many riders custom-groove their own tires for specific track conditions. Unfortunately, the soft compounds used for TT tires means they get worn out fairly quickly, making tires one of the biggest race-to-race expenses for that form of racing.

Circle track ATV racing is like dirt track car racing—left-turns only on oval tracks. Riders who specialize in these types of events offset their chassis with axles and wheel spacers to get the best bite in the corners.

RIDE TO WIN
PLANNING YOUR ATTACK

Having a race strategy is almost as important as having the skills to put in a fast lap. Begin your plan by carefully watching the starting procedure. Unless your race is the first one up, you'll get a chance to watch several other classes go off the line. Watch the starter to see if he has any habits or quirks you can use to your advantage. Try to figure out what the best spot on the line is for getting the hole shot.

During practice, make sure you practice several starts off the line. Figure out exactly what gear will give you the best launch. And you'll want to note precisely where you want your weight, so you'll get the best traction without wheelying off the line. It's a fine line between being too far forward (not enough rear-wheel traction) and too far back (too much traction and a big wheelie).

The most important part of a TT or a motocross race is the start. Getting to the first turn in front of as many guys as possible gives you a big advantage. Having to pass a lot of people requires a lot of energy and allows the leaders to get that much further ahead of you.

Once the race has started, you'll want to pace yourself so you'll still have some energy left at the end. This strategy is quite different depending on whether you're racing TT, MX, or cross country, but after having a few races under your belt you'll have a good idea of what your physical limits are and will be able to adjust accordingly.

Choosing a place on the track to make a clean pass is something that the top guys are really good at. Carefully watch the rider in front of you and try to figure out what part of the track he's a bit slower on and you can catch him. Always be looking for and trying other lines as you get him in your sights. As the laps wind down, really pour it on at the finish and pick off the guys and gals who wore themselves out.

SAND AND DIRT DRAGS

Out West and near dune riding areas, ATV dragsters race on sand. In the southern states, dirt drags rule. These short tracks, ranging from 300 feet to one-eighth of a mile, run two quads heads up against each other just like the NHRA (National Hot Rod Association) drags. Most tracks even have a Christmas tree and electronic timing lights.

Depending on the class you're in, the modifications can range from pure stock to anything goes. Some of the really wild quad dragsters feature lightweight aftermarket frames, huge street motorcycle

During practice, make sure you perform several starts off the line. Figure out exactly what gear will give you the best launch. And you'll want to note precisely where you want your weight, so you'll get the best traction without wheelying off the line. It's a fine line between being too far forward (not enough rear-wheel traction) and too far back (too much traction and a big wheelie).

You could certainly say that ATV freestyle is a form of ATV competition. Riders get judged on their performances just like gymnasts at the Olympics. The quads are set up similar to pro-level motocross machines with special holes and grippers on the seat, grabber, and handlebars for the wild tricks the riders perform.

engines, long swingarms, narrow rear axles, and big paddle tires in the back. You'll find lots of unorganized quad drag racing at the sand dunes where they usually race up a steep, whoop-filled hill. However, many sand jamborees now feature organized drags as well.

OTHER FORMS OF ATV COMPETITIONS

Incredibly, there are even more ways to compete with your four-wheeler. There are mud runs, where riders are timed as they struggle through a deep pit filled with mud and water and ATV rodeos at county fairs. In the rodeos, quads compete in traditional favorites like the barrel race and slalom course, but also log jumps and wheelie contests. I've even seen a boulder run up a ravine once.

ATV pulls are another attraction that's big in some parts of the country. Like tractor pulls, ATVs pull a sled (scaled down for quads!) that moves a weight forward as the ATV goes down the track. The rider who goes the farthest in his or her class wins.

ANECDOTE
DO YOUR MOTO MATH

This was a tough lesson for me. When I first started racing motocross, I didn't do my moto math and it cost me the win. It was a typical two-moto format, and I won the first moto and was set to take the overall trophy. However, I never looked at the sheet to see how the rest of the guys finished. I got the hole shot in the second moto and led most of the race. A rider tried to pass me with a couple of laps to go and I battled him hard. We eventually tangled and I flipped over while he continued on for the win.

Afterwards, my racing buddy knocked me upside the head and told me I should have just let that guy pass. He said the rider who passed me finished fourth in the first moto, and there's no way he could have beaten me for the overall if he won and I finished second. So before the second moto, you should always figure out which riders you have to beat to get a trophy and which ones you can let pass. Take a good look at their numbers and machines so you can spot them while you're racing (your crew with a pit board can help you in those situations as well).

ATV pulls are quite popular at ATV jamborees, festivals, and county fairs. Just like tractor pulls, the quads pull a sled (down-sized for ATVs) with a moving weight that makes it heavier the further they go. There are usually classes for both stock machines as well as super-modified quads.

And finally, one of the neatest kinds of ATV competition is a beach race. There are only a couple of places in this country where beach races are held, while in Europe there are several famous ones that draw huge numbers of riders and spectators. The temporary beach race courses are generally like a motocross track and can be short or long, depending on how much beach area they have to work with.

ATV RACING AT A GLANCE

TYPE OF RACING	MACHINE PREP	KEYS TO WINNING
Motocross	Faster Engine Better suspension	Top physical condition Great starts Jumping ability Passing ability
TT/Short Track	Faster engine Lowered chassis Slick tires	Great starts Consistent cornerin Passing ability
Cross Country	Dependable, fast engine Chassis protection Tough tires and rims	Endurance Pacing yourself Riding smart Tight woods ability Tackling hillclimbs
Desert/Endurance	Dependable, fast engine Taller suspension More fuel load Tough tires and rims	Endurance Pacing yourself Riding smart Handling sandy whoops
Ice Racing	Fast engine Lowered chassis Studded tires	Great starts Consistent cornering Passing ability
Hillclimbs	Fast engine Lengthened swingarm Paddle tires	Hillclimbing ability Jumping ability
Dirt/Sand Drags	Fast engine Lengthened swingarm Paddle tires	Great starts

Dirt and sand drag racing are a fun and easy form of ATV competition to participate in. The tracks are typically 300 feet long, and there are usually classes for just about every type of machine and rider.

MAINTAINING FOR RELIABILITY
TREAT YOUR ATV WELL AND IT WON'T LET YOU DOWN

Chapter 12

HERE WE WILL COVER

- **Routine maintenance**

- **Drivetrain and chassis care**

- **Long-term storage**

- **Cleaning and cosmetics**

- **Easy air filter care**

Racers are always double-checking their mechanical components. Trail riders don't have do it as often, but it wouldn't hurt!

Just like a car or a boat, your quad is going to need some regular maintenance to stay healthy. Most new ATVs come with a recommended maintenance schedule in the owner's manual. Of course, if most of your riding is in extra-tough conditions, such as mud or heavy hauling, you may want to perform some of the maintenance chores more often than recommended.

There are quite a few of these tasks you'll be able to handle on your own if you're fairly competent with basic tools. Luckily, the chores that have to be done the most often also happen to be among the easiest to perform.

If you're more mechanically inclined, you can save a lot of money by doing some of the bigger jobs yourself. No matter what brand or year your four-wheeler is, you can usually find an in-depth repair manual (also known as a factory shop manual) for your specific machine. There are several different companies that make ATV shop manuals. These books are a must if you plan to tackle any major repairs or maintenance. A good

selection of factory and aftermarket service manuals is available at www.repairmanuals.com.

Below are some tips and advice on both the little and big jobs when it comes to ATV maintenance and repair.

OIL

- The simple procedure of checking the oil on your ATV can be quite different depending on the model. Some require that you screw the dipstick back in to check the oil level, while others have you sticking it in without screwing it in at all. That can make a big difference in the reading! Check your owner's manual to find the right procedure for your quad.
- Synthetic oils are more expensive than petroleum-based oils, but many mechanics feel that the synthetics work better in high-heat conditions.
- When changing your oil, look for metal shavings or chunks on the drain plug magnet (recess) for signs of internal troubles. When replacing the oil filter, you

Front A-arm bushings are either rubber (inside a metal sleeve) or plastic. Check for wear by putting the ATV up and grabbing the front wheel and rock it in a front-to-back motion. If the movement is excessive, the bushings will need to be replaced. Plastic bushings require occasional greasing through the zerk fittings. Pump in fresh grease until the old stuff seeps from the bushing point.

should also check it for metal debris as well.

• Spend the extra small amount of money for a new drain plug gasket or O-ring every time you change the oil. Your garage floor and oil level will thank you.

• When you add or change oil, don't overfill! This can harm the engine. When replacing oil, do it in small increments and keep checking.

• Don't over tighten the drain plug. Plugs are usually made from steel and the case is made of aluminum. Tighten with a torque wrench to the owner's manual specifications.

• Only use spin-on oil filters that are specifically made for your ATV model. Just because one from a Honda Civic might fit, don't use it. Using the wrong filter can change your oil pressure, which can end up confusing your pressure bypass valve and severely damage your engine.

• Lubricate the gasket on the oil filter before installation. Tighten by hand.

• Before you replace a cartridge-type oil filter, wipe out the oil filter housing with a clean cloth to get any leftover sludge out.

TIP

WD-40 IS YOUR FRIEND

The popular lubricant WD-40 or other similar spray-ons can be used as a lubricant, cleaner, and a polish. Your engine can be made to shine after a cleaning, but it will pick up more dust on your next ride. However, it sure makes cleaning time easy! Before a ride, mud riders coat the A-arms, swingarms, and underneath the fenders to keep the gorp from sticking.

Carefully inspecting your ATV on occasion can help prevent scenes like this. Of course, a very clean quad makes the inspection routine that much easier. Look for stress cracks, leaks, and loose fasteners.

Always check the gap on new spark plugs. A round, wire-type gapping tool works better than a flat feeler gauge.

AIR FILTERS

• See sidebar on page 130 for all the information on air filters, as well as the step-by-step procedures for cleaning and changing.

COOLANT

• A mixture of 50 percent water and 50 percent coolant, or anti-freeze, is the correct fluid for water-cooled OHV engines. Change your coolant at least every two years to avoid corrosion in the system.

SPARK PLUGS

• Spark plugs wear out quicker on ATVs than they do on cars (the gap grows wider). As plugs wear, gas mileage and performance will drop. You will know if the plug has been ignored for too long, as the engine will start to sputter and miss under a load.
• Avoid removing plugs from a hot engine because this can damage the threads in the aluminum cylinder head. By the same token, always thread the spark plug by hand because they are very easy to cross thread.

Place a thin coating of anti-seize on the thread to help with removal the next time.
• Always check the gap on new spark plugs. A round, wire-type gapping tool works better than a flat feeler gauge.
• At every tune-up, visually check the spark plug cable for burns cuts or breaks in the insulation. Check the boot and nipple on the coil. Replace any damaged wiring.

VALVES AND IGNITIONS

• With the higher-quality metals and components used in modern ATV engines, the need for periodic valve adjustments has been reduced. Consult your owner's manual for valve lash specifications and a good shop manual will walk you through all the steps.
• Don't worry about ignition timing. All modern ATVs have electronic ignitions and adjusting them is no longer recommended.

CARBURETORS

• Before attempting to adjust the carburetor, make sure your troubles are not

Pre-filters, or "skins," are the best innovation in the filter business since the two-stage foam units came along. Three companies make them: Outerwears Pre-Filters, K&N Pre-chargers, and PC Racing's Filterskins. They slip over the air filter and catch the largest contaminants before they even get to the real filter. There are specific pre-filters built for water-resistance or extra-fine dust.

with the air filter, fuel lines, bad gas, cables, plugs, ignition, or valves.

• Some carburetors on certain ATVs have been fitted with tamper-resistant screws to prevent adjustment to the air/fuel mixtures. You will only be able to adjust the idle.

• Throttle cables can stretch over time. Adjust it at the throttle cable housing (right next to the thumb throttle) to get a free-play of 5–10 millimeters. The cable and cam near the carburetor should occasionally be lubricated.

TRANSMISSIONS: CLUTCHES AND DRIVESHAFTS

• Most four-stroke ATV transmissions share their oil with the engine. Those that don't require special oil for the gears.

• Manual clutch cables need to be adjusted periodically. Too much free play in the cable causes clutch drag (lurching forward with the clutch pulled in) and not enough free play results in clutch slippage.

• Many ATVs today feature a belt-drive automatic transmission. Periodically, check

Most four-stroke ATV transmissions share their oil with the engine. Those that don't require special oil for the gears.

ATVs are tough, but there is such a thing as abuse. Keep stunts like this up and you'll bend some expensive parts (as well as pay for a trip to the chiropractor).

TIP
AVOID HEADACHES
BY ORGANIZING

Veteran mechanics know that the key to putting everything back together again is to have all the parts laid out in an organized manner. Use small boxes to keep the various parts and hardware separated, and pay careful attention to the order that springs, washers, and bolts go by laying them on shop rags in sequence. If you don't, you may end up wasting lots of time just trying to figure it out.

the belt for signs of wear, fraying, or cracking. A broken belt on the trail means you're out of commission for the day.

• The shaft-drives on ATVs don't require much maintenance. Some of the drive shafts, in fact, are permanently lubricated and sealed. The others do require occasional oil changes (check your manual) and checking to make sure the oil level is correct.

CHAINS AND SPROCKETS

• Most models now come with permanently lubricated O-ring chains that last much longer and require less maintenance than conventional chains. Just because you have

an O-ring chain doesn't mean it still doesn't need occasional cleaning and lubrication in order to fight wear and corrosion.

• Use a stiff wire brush and a suitable solvent (kerosene works well) to clean the chains and the sprockets. Mud is the biggest enemy of chains and sprockets. There are some special devices designed specifically for cleaning and lubricating your chain drive.

• Any sprockets showing damage or wear should be replaced because they will also wear out your chain. Hooked teeth on the sprocket are signs of excessive wear.

• When lubricating a chain with a spray lubricant, spray the *inside* (sprocket side) of

the chain. That is where most of the metal-to-metal contact is and it works the lubricant to the outside of the chain rather than just flinging it off.

• New chains normally stretch and need to be adjusted for slack. Check your owner's manual for proper slack. A very important thing to remember when making chain adjustments is to always turn the adjusters the same on each side of the swingarm to preserve the alignment of the rear axle.

• After adjusting the slack, check the chain once more for stretch by pulling the chain off the rear sprocket with your fingers. If you can see more than half of the tooth, the chain is too stretched and should be replaced.

TIRES AND WHEELS

• Tires can be permanently damaged (stretched) if over inflated. Be especially careful with high-pressure air pumps. ATV tires are generally run with very low tire pressures. Check with the owner's manual for your tire pressure specs.

• If your ATV doesn't come with one (or if you've broken, or misplaced yours), get a low-pressure gauge. Most pressure gauges start at five pounds or more and are not very accurate in their lower reaches. An advantage of a commercial gauge over one that comes in the tool kit is that they usually read higher pressures than the seven pounds of the freebie one, which is useful if you ride in the desert or in high-speed rocky conditions where you might need more pressure.

• Make sure the tire pressures are all the same. A difference of just one pound from one side to other may make the ATV pull to one side.

• Some ATV tires are directional (the tread is built to go in one direction), while others are not. You can tell if there are arrows stamped on the side of the tire.

• Most ATV wheels are slightly offset. Some riders flip-flop the wheels to gain more width at the axle. Your valve stems, however, will be on the inside of the rim; make sure it clears the brakes, suspension, etc.

Check rear axle bearings by putting your quad on a stand and grabbing a rear wheel, rocking it back and forth to look for sloppiness. Some rear axle hubs have grease fittings for easy bearing lubrication.

If your ATV doesn't come with one (or if you've broken, or misplaced yours), get a low-pressure gauge. Most pressure gauges start at five pounds or more and are not very accurate in their lower reaches.

Don't worry about ignition timing. All modern ATVs have electronic ignitions and adjusting them is no longer recommended.

You can check brake fluid levels on most ATVs by eyeing the sight glass on the handlebar reservoir.

• Check the wheels for dents, cracks, gouges, and missing chunks. A scraped-up wheel may just be unsightly, but a wheel with a missing chunk or a bend that exposes the tire bead is dangerous.

• Check for bent wheels by spinning the wheels with the quad off the ground; look for excessive side-to-side or up and down movement, as if the wheel has an egg shape.

• When installing wheels, it's a good idea to apply a small amount of anti-seize paste to the mounting surfaces between the wheel and the hub.

• Torque lug nuts to the proper specs to keep them from becoming loose and to avoid hub assembly warpage from uneven tightening.

• Some riders, such as racers who change a lot of tires, use a bead-breaking tool to get the job done. Most recreational riders have the chore done by their dealers or buy their new tires with new rims.

BRAKES

• You can check brake fluid levels on most ATVs by eyeing the sight glass on the handlebar reservoir. Make sure the handlebars are turned in the manner described in your owner's manual when checking.

• Don't mix different types of DOT brake fluid. Most four-wheelers today require a DOT 3 or DOT 4 fluid.

• Mushy hydraulic brakes will require brake bleeding to remove the air that is causing the problem (usually due to a low fluid level or a hose or line that has been disconnected). Gravity bleeding is the easiest but takes some time. Simply attach a hose to the bleeder nipple and place the open end in a container (brake fluid is nasty stuff—keep it away from pets and children!). Open the bleeder nipple and let the fluid flow out. Keep the reservoir topped off and check the progress from time to time.

• Periodically check brake hoses and lines for damage or seepage. When replacing brake lines and hoses, make sure they are the same length to avoid problems with routing or performance.

• Disc brake systems require little maintenance other than an occasional

CLEANING AND COSMETICS
WASHING, PLASTIC REPAIR, AND PAINTING

Washing an ATV is actually pretty easy. However, there are many handy tips that will help you do a better job of it. In the first place, don't use a high-pressure cleaning wand because that can force water past seals and gaskets and into lubricants and other areas not tolerant of water. Use only a low-pressure garden hose or equivalent to remove mud and dirt.

Don't let water get into the end of the exhaust either. A piece of duct tape will do the trick. Also, try not to directly spray at electrical connections. Carefully clean the radiator or cooling fins with the hose; mud left in there to dry will decrease their effectiveness. You can use a toothpick to carefully pry out small rocks in radiators.

The more mud and dirt you can hose off before washing with a towel the better because that will decrease the chance of scratching the plastic with the grit. Soak your towels in a sudsy wash solution (car wash soap works best, but dish soap works fine as well) and dunk the cloth frequently to rinse out the dirt. Biodegradable degreasers work well for the engine and frame areas, but heavy-duty engine degreasers can stain your plastic.

Brushes of different types and sizes make great tools for hard-to-reach places. However, make sure the bristles aren't so stiff that they'll scratch the plastic or damage seals or rubber boots.

There are several products available that can help smooth out scratched plastic fenders. Any well-stocked auto parts store or your local ATV dealer should carry plastic polishes and scratch remover. Some scratch removers are designed for big, deep gouges as well.

The painted metal surfaces on your ATV are not merely for looks; the paint keeps rust at bay. Four-wheelers take quite a beating on the trail and you'll soon be seeing lots of scratches and nicks on the painted surfaces. Touching-up the bad spots will keep the rust from creeping under the paint and causing bigger problems.

To start the touch-up process, thoroughly clean the affected area and sand down to the bare metal any rust that has developed. Apply an anti-rust primer or rust converter, or the rust could make its way back to the surface after painting. Then apply by brush or spray the best-matched paint color you can find.

Rubber items on your ATV, such as lever boots or shaft-drive boots, can be spruced up with a light coating of a rubber and vinyl treatment. This will keep the rubber moist and supple and will slow down the cracking and aging process. Don't spray it on your grips, though!

Aluminum parts are much more resistant to corrosion than steel and some of these parts are left unpainted. However, it can get oxidized, which can be detected by a whitish dust on the surface. This can be removed with a scouring pad or, in tougher cases, sandpaper. Aluminum polishes can really make bare aluminum parts shine with a little elbow grease. Don't use the polish on coated aluminum surfaces (paint, anodized, or powder coat) as this will seriously damage the finish. Some aluminum parts have a clear coat on them and it's hard to tell whether it's bare or not. Check with someone who knows if you're a bit confused on this.

Seats can be kept clean and supple with an occasional application of a vinyl and plastic treatment. Give it time to soak in before you go riding or you may slip off!

When reassembling components, try to adhere to the recommended torque specifications.

ALL ABOUT AIR FILTERS
THE MOST IMPORTANT MAINTENANCE CHORE ON YOUR ATV

Air filters are both your engine's best friend and its worst enemy. When they're working properly and getting regular cleaning, an air filter will help your engine live a long healthy life and keep it breathing for maximum performance. However, when they fail or don't get cleaned very often, air filters can turn into the biggest ATV engine killers. In fact, nearly any ATV shop owner will tell you that the number one cause of ATV engine damage is when sand, dirt, and water get past the air filter system and get sucked into the cylinder.

Unlike on an automobile, ATV air filters are constantly having lots of crud thrown their way despite their hidden location underneath the seat.

Fortunately for us, the steps for cleaning and maintaining air filters isn't that difficult, especially after you've done it a few times. And today, there's also a myriad of aftermarket filters to choose from, as well as a new generation of filter skins that greatly enhance the performance and longevity of each filter application.

Below is the step-by-step filter cleaning procedure. Along with this are some tried-and-true air filter tips that cover just about everything you need to know about this important, but somewhat neglected, aspect of off-road riding.

FIVE EASY STEPS
CLEAN IT: To make this entire process more pleasant, begin by donning a pair of cheap disposable plastic gloves. Next, remove your air filter from the quad, being extremely careful not to knock any dirt into the intake boot (a little chunk of dirt in the carb at this point will cancel out the entire reason for cleaning the filter in the first place). There are several ways to clean foam filters. The best is to use a spray can of good-quality foam filter cleaner (a simple grease-cutting dishwashing detergent and warm water works fine too). Spray it on and let it sit for a few minutes to loosen up all the dirt and oil. Then rinse out the filter under warm water, making sure the water flows only from the inside out. Running water on the outside of the filter will force the dirt farther into the filter, rather than out.

To do a really thorough job, you can take the next step of dipping the filter into another cleaner such as Twin Air Liquid Dirt Remover, but washing with the first cleaner usually is enough. Hold the filter up to the light periodically and check for dirt. If you still see contamination, give it another rinse. If foam filter cleaners aren't available, washing the filter with soap and warm water works, but may take more elbow grease.

DRY IT: This next step is one that many riders forget about. You have to let the filter air dry before you apply the oil. Don't use a heat source such as a hair dryer; this can damage the filter. A damaged air filter will pass dirt, and that's the last thing you want for your motor.

Once it's dry, inspect it for any tears and to see if the seams are starting to separate. Air will flow through the path of least resistance, and a tear will be it.

OIL IT: Don't use plain old motor oil! Always use a quality foam filter oil. The easiest way to oil a foam filter is to pour some oil into a sealable plastic bag and add the filter. Work the oil thoroughly into the filter, making sure you get it into every nook and cranny. There are also spray-on oils for filters. You still have to work the filter rigorously to make sure the oil has penetrated throughout the filter.

LET IT SIT: After oiling, it's best to let the filter sit overnight before installing. This will allow the excess oil to drain, and you can inspect it to make sure there are no dry spots. If you didn't let the filter dry completely after cleaning, there may have been some water left, and oil doesn't mix with water. This will result in un-oiled spots on the filter when the water evaporates—not a good thing!

REINSTALL: Before reinstalling, clean any dirt or crud that has accumulated in the air box with a clean rag, always being careful not to knock any junk into the intake boot (some mechanics stuff a clean rag in the boot whenever the filter is off). When reinstalling, be sure to not let any dirt get on the inside of your filter after you cleaned it.

If any dirt gets in there, don't try brushing it off; re-clean the filter. All it takes is a surprisingly small amount of dirt to damage the piston and cylinder. If the filter foam seats against the air box itself, spread a layer of high-temperature grease on the portion of the filter that mates with the air box and you are set. As you can see, cleaning your air filter is not that difficult, and after a few times it will seem as easy as airing up the tires. A clean air filter has been proven over and over again to be the best thing you can do to keep your quad living a long and healthy life.

THINGS YOU MAY NOT KNOW ABOUT FILTERS
• All air filters are not made the same. There are lots of aftermarket filters to choose from and in almost every instance they are more efficient and longer-lasting than the stock units, and the price difference isn't even worth worrying about. The best foam filters are dual-stage, with a more porous outer stage and a finer inner stage. Premium aftermarket air filters, for the money, are simply the best investment you can make for your ATV.
• Don't use gasoline to clean your filter. Gas breaks down the glue that is used to bind the seams in a foam filter. Use the manufacturer's specified cleaning system (like Twin Air's cleaner and cleaning tub setup) to insure long filter life.
• After washing, a filter needs time to dry and additional time for the distribution solvent to evaporate. Having more than one filter means you'll always have one ready to

continued on next page

install and will be less likely to neglect this important part of your quad's maintenance routine

• Don't use motor oil! A good-quality filter oil has two components not found in plain old motor oil. A water-like solvent aids in dispersing the oil evenly (it evaporates after about 12 hours). Another component, which you can call "stickiness," keeps the oil suspended in the filter, preventing it from draining to the bottom and dripping off.

• If you think adding less oil will get better airflow, you're wrong! A properly oiled filter does not significantly reduce airflow. Without enough oil, dirt can pass through and then you'll have bigger problems than better airflow.

• Despite what you may think, it's the oil, rather than the filter, that actually catches the dirt. That's why using the correct type of oil and in the right amount is so important.

• There is no such thing as totally clean air. Even filters for personal watercraft build up dirt and require cleaning, so don't underestimate what your ATV filter is going through.

• Pre-filters, or "skins," are the best innovation in the filter business since the two-stage foam units came along. Three companies make them: Outerwears Pre-Filters, K&N Pre-chargers, and PC Racing's Filterskins. They slip over the air filter and catch the largest contaminants before they even get to the real filter. There are specific pre-filters built for water-resistance or extra-fine dust.

• Many racers and dune riders use K&N filters, which differ from foam units. These filters consist layers of fiber, sandwiched between two wire screens and pleated for more surface area. Oil is also applied to this type of filter. These types of filters aren't recommended for real dusty or wet conditions, which are better handled by the foam units.

• If you ride for long periods in real dusty conditions, you should clean your air filter after every ride. Dune riders tend to pick up lots of sand, so they too need to stay on top of air filter maintenance, especially if they aren't running a pre-filter. If you ride in an environment where there isn't a lot of dust, you can get in quite a few days of riding before your filter needs cleaning.

• Don't rely solely on a visual inspection of the filter in your machine to know if it's clean. It may have taken on dust that you can't see that is working its way through the pores. In the whole scheme of things, if the filter looks at all like it's dirty, it's best to take the safe route and go ahead and clean it. Your engine will thank you in the long run.

---

check on pad wear or fluid level. To check or change the brake pads, check your owner's manual or repair manual.

• Drum brakes are becoming rare on new model ATVs. Maintain brake adjustment so that the pedal has about one inch of movement before the linings contact the drum.

• Some drum brakes have wear indicators fitted to the brake cam. In most cases, these consist of arrows. If the arrows align when the brake is applied, the brake linings are worn to the point of replacement.

• When replacing the shoes on drum brakes (check your owner's manual or repair manual for specific instructions), rough up the "glazing" on the surface of the linings (where the brakes meet) with sandpaper. You can also do this whenever you're cleaning or inspecting the drum brakes.

• Lightly grease the cam and pivot points of the brake shoes before assembly.

STEERING AND SUSPENSION

• Front A-arm bushings are either rubber (inside a metal sleeve) or plastic. Check for wear by putting the ATV up and grabbing the front wheel and rock it in a front-to-back motion. If the movement is excessive, the bushings will need to be replaced. Plastic bushings require occasional greasing through the zerk fittings. Pump in fresh grease until the old stuff seeps from the bushing point.

• Check the rubber boots on the tie-rod ball joint for cracking or splitting. A torn boot would allow dirt in and could cause premature ball-joint failure. The tie rods may or may not have grease fittings. If not, they are maintenance-free and do not require lubrication.

• The bushings or needle bearings utilized by the swingarm where it's attached to the frame are a common place for wear. To check, lift the rear wheels off the ground and grab the swingarm from the back and try to move it from side-to-side. Any play signifies a need for replacement. If your ATV is shaft-driven, there may be a requirement for special tools to remove the rear swingarm from the frame (check your owner's manual or repair manual).

• Check tie rods by grabbing and twisting the front wheels from side-to-side. If there is any clunking or play, they are worn out and should be replaced. Grabbing the wheel and rocking it vertically (assuming the wheel bearings are in good condition) will test the spindle for any excessive

Most ATVs require a small amount of toe-in (meaning the front wheels point inward slightly) or in some cases, no toe at all.

Check tie rods by grabbing and twisting the front wheels from side-to-side. If there is any clunking or play, they are worn out and should be replaced. Grabbing the wheel and rocking it vertically (assuming the wheel bearings are in good condition) will test the spindle for any excessive clearance.

clearance. Usually, spindles are not adjustable and will require replacement if they are found to be worn.

• To check the alignment of the front end, stand the ATV up on end and set the handlebars straight. Most ATVs require a small amount of toe-in (meaning the front wheels point inward slightly) or in some cases, no toe at all. Measure the front edge of the wheel and the rear edge to calculate how much toe-in you have and compare it to what is listed in the owner's manual. Change the toe-in by adjusting the tie rods.

• Most ATVs have some basic form of adjusting the shocks for a softer or stiffer ride. With you aboard, and the suspension adjusted properly, the ATV should sit down one-third of the total length of the suspension travel. For example, if the total suspension travel of your ATV is around nine inches, the shocks should be compressed about three inches with you on board. This will allow your shocks to work in both directions as you ride.

• To set the correct preload on most stock ATV shocks (the tension on the springs), use a spanner wrench (which is usually

When you have the top-end off your machine, keep it covered! A small screw or nut accidentally dropped in could ruin the entire engine. Dirt and grime doesn't help matters either.

included in the tool kit) to change the notched adjusters. Some shocks feature threaded adjusters with two rings.

• The only periodic maintenance required for shocks is a visual inspection for oil leaks or an oily residue. That would indicate a broken seal and the shock would need to be replaced.

• Wheel bearings on ATVs take a lot of abuse. Most are sealed, but if you ride in a lot of mud and water, junk can still get in there and wear out the bearings. Check by rocking the front and rear wheels from side-to-side with the wheels off the ground (the suspension and steering linkages should be in top condition because you could easily mistake a worn-out ball joint or tie rod for a bad wheel bearing).

• Check rear axle bearings by putting your quad on a stand and grabbing a rear wheel, rocking it back and forth to look for sloppiness. Servicing the rear axle bearings on most ATVs requires the use of special tools and many riders have the work done at a repair shop. Some rear axle hubs have grease fittings for easy bearing lubrication.

Wheel bearings on ATVs take a lot of abuse. Most are sealed, but if you ride in a lot of mud and water, junk can still get in there and wear out the bearings.

Disc brake systems require little maintenance other than an occasional check on pad wear or fluid level. Periodically check brake hoses and lines for damage or seepage. When replacing brake lines and hoses, make sure they are the same length to avoid problems with routing or performance.

ALERT!

WARRANTIES AND MAINTENANCE

If you have a new ATV with a manufacturer's warranty, it's extremely important that you follow all of the manufacturer's recommendations regarding care and maintenance. Keep a careful record with a logbook and receipts of chores performed, and try to use the manufacturer's recommended fluids and parts while your machine is under warranty. The first thing a dealer is going to ask you when you come in with a problem is if you've been keeping up with the recommended maintenance.

CONTROL CABLES, SHIFTERS, AND BATTERIES

• Water can get into the throttle mechanism and cables and cause troubles. Occasionally inspect the throttle mechanism and make sure the gasket is in good shape. A simple cable lubrication tool will help you get things running smoothly again. Also check the rubber boots at cable junctures for tears that may shorten cable life.

• Do not lubricate Teflon-lined cables as the cable is designed to be self-lubricating. You may have to check your owner's manual or with your dealer to find out if your ATV has Teflon cables.

• The majority of control cables have some form of adjustment to compensate for the natural stretching of the cable and wear of parts, like brake shoes. When you run out of adjustments at both ends of the cable, it's time to replace the cables (or the brakes).

• When replacing a cable, always make sure it is routed properly. Once the cable is replaced, turn the handlebars from side-to-side and check for any problems.

• Any linkage on a four-wheeler, including the handlebar levers and shifter linkage, need to be lubricated on a regular basis. Lubrication of shifter linkage and brake linkage is essential for safe operation, as well as preventing excessive wear.

• Apply oil or light grease to all bushings and sliding surfaces. Anti-seize compound can also be used.

• Nearly all batteries in today's ATVs are sealed, non-maintenance units. If it goes

dead and needs recharging, don't use the same charger you use for your car! There are special chargers for small motorcycle and ATV batteries.

• Make sure when replacing a battery that it is the same physical size and provides the same power output.

LONG-TERM STORAGE

• Clean your ATV thoroughly and then protect the various surfaces of the ATV before placing it in storage (see sidebar in this chapter for cleaning tips).

• Over time, the most volatile components in gasoline evaporates, leaving the fluid less combustible. This will lead to difficult starting and a rough-running engine.

• As gas evaporates, it leaves behind a varnish that can coat and clog the fuel delivery system.

• You have two choices for the fuel problems listed above: Before storing, completely drain the fuel system or add a

fuel stabilizer. Which one you choose depends on how long your four-wheeler is going to be stored. If it's in years rather than months, drain the system. Otherwise a fuel stabilizer will do the job.

• When adding a fuel stabilizer, it is best to pour the stabilizer into the tank first and then add the gas. Top off the tank to minimize the amount of air. Next, fire up your ATV and run it for a while to allow the fuel/stabilizer mix to reach all parts of the system.

• If your engine coolant is getting close to the time for a change, do it before your ATV goes into storage, especially if it's going to be stored in subfreezing temperatures. As coolant ages, it looses its ability to prevent freezing and that can seriously damage your engine.

• A small amount of water that normally accumulates in the engine or transmission oils is typically heated up and evaporates as the quad is running. However, during

With the higher-quality metals and components used in modern ATV engines, the need for periodic valve adjustments has been reduced. Consult your owner's manual for valve lash specifications, and a good shop manual will walk you through all the steps.

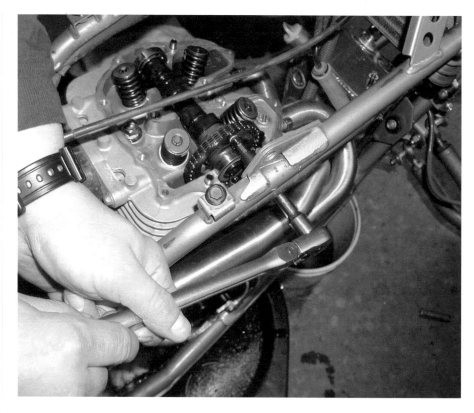

Manual clutches can be abused and burnt up. Replacing them isn't a very difficult chore. You will probably want to opt for an aftermarket heavy-duty clutch.

storage the water can condense and cause corrosion. The safe bet is to change all your oils before long-term storage. The same can be said for brake fluids.

• A fresh coating of chain lubrication will protect that part of the drivetrain.

• A smart charger or battery tender (a device which maintains a proper charge without overcharging) will keep your battery fresh throughout the storage. An occasional cycle from a trickle charger works as well. If your quad is going to be stored in very cold temperatures, remove the battery and bring into a warmer area for winter.

• Properly inflate the tires, and if possible store the quad on a lift to prevent "flat spots" from forming.

• When you pull your quad out of storage, check for rodent nests in the air box or muffler! If you see evidence of rodents, double-check all hoses and electrical wires.

Big jobs may require that you remove all of the plastic. Look how much easier it's going to be to work on this sand dragster!

TIP

DIRTY AIR FILTERS ARE AN ATV's DEADLIEST ENEMY

Virtually every ATV mechanic will tell you that the number one cause of engine wear and tear are riders who don't keep their air filter clean or properly installed. Even small grit like dust will get into an engine and wear it out before its time. Cleaning your air filter isn't that difficult and once you make it a regular chore it becomes even easier. In addition, dirty air cleaners waste gas and rob horsepower.

TROUBLESHOOTING AND FIELD REPAIRS

WHAT TO DO WHEN IT WON'T START OR YOU HAVE A BREAKDOWN

HERE WE WILL COVER

- Engine woes
- Transmission troubles
- Electrical gremlins
- Chassis conundrums
- Drown-out recovery
- Do ATVs float?
- Field repairs

The biggest enemy of your ATV engine is dust. Clean your air filter on a regular basis and you'll avoid many of the scenarios detailed in this chapter.

As with any mechanical device, there will come a day when you go to use your ATV and it won't start. Or it will start and then sputter and die. Or perhaps, something in the drivetrain or transmission is malfunctioning. Whatever the problem, the solution is called "troubleshooting." This is a tried-and-true method of diagnosis, whereby you'll be testing and evaluating the various systems and components of your ATV in a search for the problem area.

Once you've discovered the source of the problem, the solution is usually straightforward. To begin with, let's take a look at the basic tenants of ATV troubleshooting and then we'll get into more details on the causes of common ATV troubles.

SUCCESSFUL TROUBLESHOOTING TIPS

- Keep it simple! Always check the easier things first, working towards the more complex.
- Never assume that a system or component is working properly. Verify it!

- Check only one area at a time and don't move on to something else until you've eliminated the system or component as the cause for your problem.
- If you become frustrated, take a breather and walk away from the problem for a while. Don't allow your emotion to control your logic.
- When in doubt, always refer to the proper repair instruction manuals for information and guidance.

ENGINE WON'T START

The reasons for a "won't start" problem can be caused by a wide variety of individual or combinations of concurrent problems and the best place to begin is to do a quick check of the engine. Here are the questions you need to answer:

- Is the on/off switch turned on?
- Is the transmission in neutral?
- Is the choke in the correct position?
- Is the fuel valve turned on?
- Is the battery dead?

If your machine starts sputtering and missing while crossing streams, then you probably need to either get a new waterproof spark plug cap or apply dielectric grease to the spark plug boot. You should be able to find the grease in any auto parts store. Most ATVs are incredibly waterproof, but some water still sneaks in to cause troubles now and then.

• Is the tank full of fresh gasoline?
• Does the air filter need to be cleaned or replaced?
• What's the condition of the spark plug?
• Once you've answered those, check the oil for correct fill level and quality. If the problem isn't located or resolved during the quick check procedure, you'll need to check for the following problems:
• No ignition spark (check by pulling out plug, reattaching cap, and turning engine over while grounding plug against engine case).
• Improper timing.
• Fuel mixture not reaching the combustion chamber.
• Abnormally low compression.
• Engine not turning fast enough to start.
Suggested troubleshooting order:
Fuel, Ignition, Timing, Compression

ENGINE HARD TO START

Again, if an engine is difficult to start (may rev, but dies before fully engaging) a wide variety of individual or combinations of concurrent problems could be present. So the best place to begin is to do a quick check of the engine. Here are the items to note:
• Is the tank full of fresh gasoline?
• Does the air filter need to be cleaned or replaced?
• Check the condition of the spark plug.
• Is the fuel valve turned on?
• Is the choke in the correct position?
• Check the oil for correct fill level and quality.
• If the problem isn't located or resolved during the quick check procedure, you'll need to check for the following problems:

• Improper air mixture reaching the carb.
• Weak spark.
• Improper timing.
• Low compression.
• Not turning fast enough to start.
Suggested troubleshooting order:
Fuel, Ignition, Timing, Compression

STARTS BUT DIES QUICKLY

This situation is almost always related to a fuel system problem. So first, you should check for water in the fuel tank, hoses, and fuel bowl on the carb. If water is found, be sure to check your fuel can as well! Next check for a major air leak from around the intake or carb mounting area. If this problem occurs only during cold starts, you may also have a situation where the choke is not working properly.

The rougher you are on your quad, the greater chance of having mechanical problems. Fortunately, ATV engines and chassis are not overly complicated and many repairs can be done at home.

Even though your ATV stays relatively clean while riding in the sand, it can still take a toll on your machine when sand works its way into bearings and bushings, causing problems over time. The best way to avoid a malfunction is to take your quad apart now and then and inspect for premature wear.

TIP

DEALING WITH FLATS ON THE TRAIL

One of the most frustrating, and common, trail problems is getting a flat tire. Fortunately, a tire repair kit with CO_2 cartridges or a small pump should get you out of trouble fairly quickly and easily. You can fix a surprisingly bad tear with those plugs that you stick into the hole with glue; depending on the size of the hole, you might have to use a few plugs to make an adequate seal.

While some riders continue to run tires with plugged sidewalls for a full season, it's not a good idea. The plugged tire will get you out of the bush, but the tire should be replaced once you're back home.

A drowned-out ATV doesn't mean you're done for the day. Check out the step-by-step drownout fix on page 142.

Play in the deep water and chances are good you'll have a complete drown-out some time. The fix isn't that difficult, but you'll probably need to change the oil when you get home. One way to get water out of the cylinder is to tip the ATV up on the grabbar and let it drain out the exhaust.

• Finally, don't forget to check the fuel cap to make sure it's venting properly. A cap that doesn't vent properly will not allow fuel to flow from the tank to the carb.

THE ENGINE RUNS ROUGH AT IDLE

Any engine-related problem that can be described "runs rough" can have a variety of common causes, including the following:

• Dirty air filter.
• Weak ignition spark.
• Worn or fouled spark plug.
• Improper carb adjustment.
• Valves need adjustment.

If a full tune-up (including valve adjustments) has been performed recently and the condition is only noticed when the engine is at idle, the problem is likely to be

TIP

FROZEN CHOKE BLUES

Some ATVs feature electronic fuel injection, and a few hits usually get things going. Otherwise, if you feel the choke is frozen, remove the spark plug and pour a small amount of fuel down the hole. Replace the spark plug and hit the starter. You may have to do this three or four times, but the engine should kick over.

Once it's running, be sure to warm it up completely before taking off. When you're ready to roll, check the brakes and belt to remove any ice buildup. And next time you're out in the cold, park the quad with the choke in the open position. Also, take into account that you'll use about a third more gas in cold weather than in warm.

Over time and rough use (such as motocross racing) major components such as A-arms can break. Sometimes you get a warning that the component is about to break when you spot stress cracks in the paint.

WHAT TO DO IF YOU DROWN YOUR ATV
HOW TO GET THE WATER OUT AND GET RUNNING AGAIN

Anytime you're running in really deep water, or just splashing through shallower water, you run the risk of incurring a "drownout." Usually, you'll be able to get up and running again after performing drownout fixes, even if your quad was totally submerged or turned upside down in the water. There can be just one cause for a drownout (such as a wet stator), or, in most cases, a combination of a whole bunch of things (water in the air box, cylinder, and exhaust). By taking the following step-by-step approach, you can systematically eliminate each one of the troubles and get going again in a fairly short amount of time:

STEP-BY-STEP RESUSCITATION

1. Pull the ATV out of the water. Pop the lid off the air box to see if that's where the trouble originated. If the air box is soaked, pull out the spark plug, dry it off and set it aside. If possible, dry out the spark plug cap with a dry cloth. If the air filter is soaked, remove it and wring it out.

2. If your quad is powered by a four-stroke engine, turn the on/off switch off and hit the electric start or kick the piston through, and watch all the water from the cylinder and exhaust blow out through the pipe. If water keeps coming out of the exhaust, stand it up on the grab bar and let it drain out. If your machine is a two-stroke, with the plug removed, tilt the ATV on its side or upside down and push the kick starter several times to drain the water out of the cylinder and bottom end through the spark plug hole (you may find that two-stroke engines can hold a surprising amount of water).

3. Drain the float bowl. If you suspect 25that water got into the gas tank (you really have to sink a quad to do that), let the machine sit upright for a few minutes so the water can settle to the bottom of the tank. Then turn the fuel petcock to reserve and drain some gas out (reserve takes fuel from the very bottom of the tank).

4. Once all the water is out of the system, replace the spark plug and air filter, pull on the choke, and try to start it. It will probably blubber and sputter, but don't hit the throttle to try to dry it out! Just let the engine idle—if you rev an engine with water in it, you can cause serious internal damage. After a few minutes of idling, the engine should start drying itself out and sounding better. If it isn't running at all, proceed to Step 5; otherwise skip to the When You Get Home after a Drownout section below.

5. If none of the above has worked, either an electrical connection or the starter has gotten wet (the CDI boxes on most quads are usually completely sealed). If you have the tools, remove the flywheel cover to see if the starter is wet. If it is, dry it off. If not, start blowing out all the electrical connections. If your quad still won't fire, and it's beginning to get dark, start pushing!

WHEN YOU GET HOME
AFTER A DROWNOUT

• Check all fluids (crankcase, tranny, shaft, front four-wheel drive). If any of the oil is milky, change it. Clean the air filter.

• Grease the heck out of everything you can (if you have zerks, blow out all the old grease completely). Lube all your cables with a light oil (don't use chain lube). Disassemble, clean, and lube just about every part you have time for.

• Pull the flywheel cover off and spray down the starter with contact cleaner or WD-40. The next time you ride, check all the fluids again when you are done; the oil may still be milky from remaining water. In that case, change the oil again.

caused by debris in the carb or an improper idle adjustment.

BASIC IDLE MIXTURE ADJUSTMENT

With the engine warmed up and running at the recommended idle speed, locate the idle mixture screw. From here, follow these steps:

• Slowly turn the idle mixture screw in clockwise until the engine just starts to miss and/or the RPM just starts to fall off.

• Turn it back out until the engine again starts to miss, hesitate, or fall off.

• Finally, again turn the mixture screw back in clockwise until you reach approximately between both extremes. Make final adjustments by turning the mixture screw no more than a fourth turn (in or out) to reach the optimum adjustment.

• While this may not be a perfect adjustment, it should suffice to solve a rough idle problem. Otherwise, if none of the other potential problems are found, you'll need to clean the carb and fuel system, paying close attention to the idle circuits in the carb.

WHITE OR BLUE/GREY SMOKE

Most people automatically associate this as a sign of a major engine problem, which is not always true. While there are definite reasons for concern, this symptom or problem is not always as bad as it appears. In fact, there are several causes for this problem that are relatively simple to troubleshoot and correct. Before you assume the worst, take a look at some of these potential causes:

• The engine has been overfilled with oil, or the oil has been contaminated with water or fuel, causing an overfilled condition. (Check the oil level, and make sure it is not contaminated.)

• Diesel fuel or two-cycle oil/fuel mix has mistakenly been added or substituted for gasoline. (Take a fuel sample in a clean container and verify that it's pure, fresh gasoline.)

• The engine has been tipped up the wrong way, causing oil to enter the combustion chamber, carburetor, and/or exhaust system. This is a very common cause for this problem. (If you have recently tipped the engine for any reason, chances are good that this will be the cause.)

• If the exhaust system or carburetor has been filled with oil, the engine will eventually stop smoking unless the air filter has become saturated with oil. If it has, the engine may not start or will run poorly until you clean or replace the air filter. Be sure to check the oil level before restarting.

Note: All of the following will require at least a partial disassembly or special tools to verify:

• The crankcase breather(s) is/are malfunctioning.

• Leaking crankcase gaskets or seals are causing the engine to lose crankcase vacuum, and allowing the oil to be "pulled" into the combustion chamber.

• Oil is leaking past worn or damaged valve stems, valve stem seals, or valve guides.

• The oil ring(s) and/or cylinder bore are worn or damaged.

If any of these are the problem, refer to the repair instruction manual or take the machine in for professional service.

BLACK SMOKE

Black smoke is always associated with an engine that is burning a very rich fuel mixture or unable to completely burn a normal amount of fuel.

Quick checks to do if this is your problem include the following:

• Check to make sure that the air filter is clean.

• Check to make sure that the spark plug isn't fouled.

• Verify that the choke control is in the off position and do a visual inspection to see that the choke valve is fully open on the carb.

• Adjust the linkage, if required.

If none of these steps indicate a problem, you may need to make adjustments to the main jet (if adjustable) or clean the fuel system and carb.

ENGINE LACKS POWER

If the engine is still relatively easy to start but lacks power, then the most probable cause is that it's time to perform routine maintenance and or a tune-up. Service or replace the air filter, replace the spark plug, and make *minor* adjustments to the carb.

Don't overlook the possibility that it could be time for a valve job. Performing a valve job and removing carbon buildup from the piston and combustion chamber occasionally should be considered to be part of normal maintenance and will insure that the engine is capable of operating at peak performance levels.

TRANSMISSION PROBLEMS

Clutch slips. *Possible causes*: Release mechanism improperly adjusted; release worm and lever sticking; clutch spring tension too loose; worn or damaged clutch springs; friction discs; or steel plates worn, warped, or oil impregnated; distorted pressure plate.

Clutch drags. *Possible causes*: Release mechanism improperly adjusted, release worm and lever or throw-out bearing excessively worn or damaged, clutch spring tension too

This freestyle jumper was doing huge leaps and broke his axle upon landing. He somehow managed to stay in the saddle. Hopefully, you won't be incurring any damage like this!

Racers have the luxury of having a pit area stocked with tons of tools and spare parts. When you're out on the trail, you'll need to bring along at least the basics to get you out of mechanical trouble and back on the ride.

What if you have a catastrophic engine breakdown? Long-distance desert racers simply do an overhaul at the next pit. On the trail, you'll need a tow from your buddy.

tight, worn or damaged clutch springs, friction discs gummy and sticking, steel plates or pressure plate warped or damaged, clutch sprocket keys excessively worn or damaged.

Transmission pops out of gear. *Possible causes:* Shifter rods or shifter forks improperly adjusted or damaged; insufficient shifter spring tension; worn or damaged gear dogs; worn transmission shaft splines; worn, damaged, or improperly adjusted shifter mechanism or linkage.

Chain whine. *Possible causes:* Chain too tight, chain rusted or kinking.

Chain slap. *Possible causes:* Chain too loose, bent chain guard.

Accelerated chain and sprocket wear. *Possible causes:* Improperly aligned sprocket or rear axle; damaged sprockets; worn, damaged, or insufficiently lubricated chain.

ELECTRICAL

Electric starter spins, but engine does not. *Possible causes:* Broken starter clutch.

Clicking sound when starter button is pushed, engine does not turn over. *Possible causes:* Low battery or battery connections loose or corroded, starter armature bushings worn.

Nothing happens when starter button is pushed. *Possible causes:* Loose or broken connections in starter switch or battery leads.

No spark or weak spark. *Possible causes:* Defective ignition coil or spark plug, plug lead or wires damaged or disconnected.

Carbon-fouled spark plug. *Possible causes:* Fuel mixture too rich, plug too cold for conditions, idle speed set too high.

Oil-fouled spark plug. *Possible causes:* Worn rings, cylinders, or valve guides (four-stroke); fuel/oil mixture incorrect (two-stroke).

Spark plug electrode burned or overheated. *Possible causes:* Plug too hot for conditions, engine overheating, ignition timing incorrect, fuel mixture too lean.

CHASSIS

Excessive vibration. *Possible causes:* Loose, broken, or worn motor mounts; loose axle nuts; excessive hub bearing play; wheels out of true or damaged; tires over inflated; tire and wheel unevenly balanced; worn steering head bearings; worn rear shock bushings or shocks; swingarm bushings too tight or too loose; excessive front end loading; cylinder head bracket loose or broken; broken or bent frame or swingarm; chain badly worn; insufficiently lubricated or too tight; incorrectly assembled clutch mechanism; excessively worn crankshaft.

Uncertain or wobbly ride. *Possible causes:* Worn or bad hub bearings, bent A-arms or swingarm, worn swingarm bushings, wheels improperly aligned, tires improperly seated on wheel, tires unevenly worn, loose front wheel, faulty right or left shock.

Pulls to one side. *Possible causes:* Incorrectly adjusted drive chain, air pressure

Kind of the like the David Letterman game of Will It Float?, I've heard many people wonder what would happen if an ATV fell into deep water. To test the theory, I rolled both a four-wheeler and a three-wheeler into a swimming pool to see what would happen.

With no rider on board, both machines turned upside down and floated due to the air in the tires. The three-wheeler floated tail-end up, while the quad was tail-end down. Since then, I've seen many photos of ATVs submerged, yet still floating, in deep water and have yet to hear about any that have completely sunk to the bottom as would a car, motorcycle, or snowmobile.

not adjusted evenly between wheels, wheels improperly aligned, incorrectly balanced tires and wheels, defective steering head bearings, bent or damaged A-arms, frame, or swingarm.

Heavy or stiff steering. *Possible causes:* Bent or damaged steering stem or frame neck, bad steering head bearings and/or races, front tire pressure too low, incorrect damper adjustment.

FLAT TIRES

If you want to be able to fix a flat on the trail, you first need to carry a plug kit on every ride. Many ATV riders don't go anywhere without one. They're cheap (about $10 at most discount or auto parts stores) and small enough to keep in a fannypack or your storage box.

Then when you discover you tire is flat or losing air, stop! You should fix the leak as soon as possible, or you risk damaging the tire or rim beyond repair. Once you locate the leak, insert the rasp tool from the plug kit to enlarge the hole and roughen up the edges. Insert the plug into the insertion tool, add the rubber cement, and push it into the hole. Some plug kits are self-vulcanizing and they work well for ATV tires as well.

Be careful not to push the plug in too far; leave half an inch or more sticking out. Then you can cut off the excess plug. Don't cut it

too short, though. If you have an extra large puncture or cut, give this a try: Insert the plug as instructed above and then have one person with a pair of pliers hold the first plug, while you add more plugs. I have seen some cuts that took six plugs to repair a slice in the sidewall. The fix wasn't pretty and not permanent, but it saved the day of riding.

Many of the top cross-country racers use a Twin-Air filter with Liquid Power Filter Oil (also available from Twin-Air). They claim it works great at keeping everything out of the air intake. If you want to simply waterproof your stock filter, add an Outerwears filter cover.

FINDING PLACES TO RIDE AND GETTING ORGANIZED
ATV CLUBS CAN BE FUN AND OPEN UP RIDING OPPORTUNITIES

HERE WE WILL COVER

- **Best ways to find ride areas**
- **Starting an ATV club**
- **How to get money for your trail project**
- **OHV advocacy groups and resources**
- **Private land riding areas**
- **Jamborees and festivals**

Is this ATV heaven or what? Finding the best places to ride can be frustrating at times, but there are many resources available to help you out.

The dealerships are a quick and easy place to begin your ride area search, but the folks who may really know about local ride areas are the ATV club members.

Once beginning ATV riders have bought their quad of choice and learned basic riding safety and techniques, they naturally have one more question they want answered: Where are the best places to ride? This chapter will answer that question, giving you some tips on how to find the best trails in your neck of the woods. One of the keys to keeping trails open in your area (as well as opening up new ones) is to have an organized front with other ATV enthusiasts. The best ways to do that are start up an ATV club and learn about the OHV advocacy and educational groups that may be able to help you with any local land-access issues you may encounter.

While it would be nice to list all of the legal riding areas in the United States here, that can't happen for two reasons: *1)* no one has ever put such a list together (there are too many different land agencies and private owners to find a list under any one banner), and *2)* there wouldn't be enough space in this book anyway. Besides, with various trail systems opening and closing each year, it

would have to be updated on a constant basis.

So how can you find a close-to-home ride area that would allow you to take a quick spin on a Saturday afternoon? Or for those big riding weekend plans, where are the best, most scenic trails in your part of the country that is worth a six- or eight-hour drive?

DEALERS AND CLUBS

Short of finding the magic know-it-all book, there are, in fact, quite a few resources to use in your quest for new trails. The best place to start is at your local dealerships. Usually the folks who work there have information on the most popular local ride areas. Often dealerships have bulletin boards and posters that tout upcoming local riding events and riding parks. Some parts of the country also have off-road newspapers that cover and list all the goings-on in the area.

The dealerships are a quick and easy place to begin your ride area search, but the folks who may really know about local ride areas are the ATV club members. The best way to get in on the good side of an ATV club is, of course, to join them! Club newsletters usually feature lists of ride areas, and in some cases the clubs even have their own privately-owned riding parks.

So how can you find out about your local club? The best resource for that is the National Off-Highway Vehicle Conservation Council (NOHVCC). The council has a huge, comprehensive list of off-highway riding clubs throughout the nation and is more than happy to put you in contact with them. Call the council at 800-348-6487, email at trailhead@nohvcc.org or check out the group's website at www.nohvcc.org that lists all the clubs and contact information.

MAPS AND BROCHURES

Federal and state government agencies that manage trail systems can also fill you in on

Guided exotic ATV expeditions have become more and more popular over the last three years. Keep an eye on the monthly magazines for articles and ads, as well as search the web for more info on these once-a-lifetime excursions into exotic locales such as South America, Mexico, Africa, and Asia.

The Glamis sand dunes area in southern California is aptly called the "World's Biggest Sandbox." Thousands of OHV enthusiasts can be found there every weekend, except in the summer months when it gets too hot.

ANECDOTE

WHERE DID THE SAND DUNES COME FROM?

Spectacular sand dunes are quite rare in this country and we're very fortunate that OHVs are allowed to recreate in many of them. Every time I go riding at Glamis in southern California, I wonder where they came from. It turns out that the most popular theory holds that the Imperial Sand Dunes (Glamis) were formed from the windblown beach sands of ancient Lake Cahuilla which covered much of the Imperial, Coachella and Mexicali valleys as late as 1450. The process continues to this day and as the dunes shift southeast at the rate of approximately one foot per year.

what they have to offer. In many cases, they'll have a brochure describing the locations of all their trails and the rules and regulations associated with them. Getting the brochure is usually pretty easy—all you need to do is give the agencies a call. To find the government agencies in your area, look in the phone book government pages under Federal Bureau of Land Management (BLM), National Forests,

Riding the big sand dunes is one of those things most ATV riders want to experience at least once. You can find sand dune riding opportunities in many of the western states, as well as the Silver Lake ride area on the western edge of Michigan.

Big gatherings of ATV riders for festivals and jamborees are a popular pastime throughout many parts of the country. Organizers jazz things up with lots of fun activities, such as ATV rodeos, guided trail rides, campouts, and barbeques.

PRIVATE LANDS ARE OPENING TO PUBLIC OHV USE
A BOON FOR LANDOWNERS, NEARBY TOWNS, AND RIDERS

Like most things, off-highway vehicle recreation in America is a constantly evolving situation. Back in the late 1960s and early '70s, when dirt bikes were first becoming popular, riders pretty much rode wherever they could get away with it—which, as it turned out, was just about everywhere! For those of us who were around back then, memories of wheelying down the middle of your street to the empty lot behind the gas station now seem pretty nostalgic. Finding places to ride was laughably easy back then.

It's certainly a much different story now. If you don't happen to have your own 40 acres of woodlands behind your house, finding a place to legally ride can be quite difficult. These days, many folks throughout the country have to trailer their OHVs several hours in order to hit the trails. Some states (mostly in the West) have huge tracts of public lands that are in many cases open to OHV recreation. Other states, such as Pennsylvania and New York, have few public lands, and guess who gets the short end of the stick when trail user groups collide? The strange thing about that is that many eastern states like Pennsylvania and New York have huge numbers of ATV owners who are thirsting for legal places to ride.

FINDING PUBLIC LANDS

A trend that has taken hold fairly recently is that more private landowners (individuals or corporations) are opening their land to OHV recreation. Sometimes fees are involved, sometimes not. Sometimes alliances are worked out with city and township governments or ATV riding clubs, who manage the areas and become the stewards and protectors of the trails. When all is said and done, most of these arrangements turn out to be quite profitable for the landowners and the nearby communities who derive lots of economic input from the visiting OHVers.

One private area that is now open for ATV use is in eastern Tennessee, on lands owned by the Coal Creek Mining and Manufacturing Company. Currently, 72,000 acres are open to OHV riding in the company's "working" forest, where some mining and logging activities are still taking place. The owners of the company worked out an agreement with a strong local organization, the Windrock ATV Club, to become partners in the venture. It has become very successful as hundreds of riders enjoying the challenging trails located near the town of Oak Ridge. All riders must purchase a permit from CCMMC for the right to ride.

A favorite ride spot on private lands for Minneapolis/ St. Paul area riders is the Arkansaw Creek Park near Arkansaw, Wisconsin, and The Big Rock ATV and Dirt Bike Park near Maysville, Kentucky, consists of nearly 2,000 acres of family-owned land. A longstanding, privately owned riding area, the Badlands Off-Road Park near Attica, Indiana, has been visited by many Midwestern OHV owners over the past decade and has proven to be very beneficial to the local economy.

Red Creek Off-Road Park in southern Mississippi is a family-owned business that offers riding for ATV, dirt bike, and 4x4 enthusiasts. A relatively new OHV park is located near the southern Illinois town of Crab Orchard. Called Little Egypt Off-Road OHV Park, it currently consists of 411 acres with another 320 acres planned for the future.

Many privately owned and operated OHV parks have gone the next step by building motocross and woods racing courses on the land. Most have relationships with local riding clubs, so several events happen each year. Some of the areas have annual memberships, camping, and other amenities that make them as attractive as riding on government-owned land.

Perhaps the biggest and best shining example of private lands being utilized by the OHV public is the massive and ever-growing Hatfield-McCoy Trail system in West Virginia. The wheels began rolling on this project way back in the early 1990s, but it wasn't until just before the new millennium that the park became a reality. It currently boasts more than 500 miles of trails in the challenging Appalachian terrain with plans to expand to 2,000 miles of trails. The list of private (mostly corporate) landowners who signed on with the architects of the trail system is huge and is still growing. Plans are that the trails will eventually spill over into Kentucky and Virginia, as well. The tremendous boost to the economies of the surrounding communities has been well documented and may well serve to inspire other parts of the country to follow suit with similar projects.

State Forests, Department of Natural Resources (DNR), Department of Parks and Recreation, Department of Tourism, Chamber of Commerce, or State Fish & Game or Fish & Wildlife. Not all of these agencies exist in all states, nor do they all necessarily have anything to do with managing off-highway trails, but if they do, they're the ones with all the maps and brochures and it's their job to give you the info.

FORMING A CLUB

Let's face it—the main driving force behind virtually every riding area that is newly opened (or saved from closing) are well-organized groups of riders. The truth is that each of us on our own doesn't really have much of a voice when it comes to the complicated and drawn-out process of opening and saving off-highway riding areas. Yet as a group—whether through coalitions,

THE BIG THREE ADVOCACY GROUPS
MAKING SENSE OF THE ATVA, BRC, AND NOHVCC

Three major off-highway vehicle organizations are dedicated to the advancement of the sport of ATV and dirt bike riding. Rather than having agendas, each one of the three organizations serves a different purpose for the recreational ATV rider.

The All-Terrain Vehicle Association (ATVA) is a direct branch of the longer-established American Motorcyclist Association (AMA). The ATVA and AMA's primary focus is at the competition and legislative end of our sport. In addition to sanctioning thousands of professional and amateur races every year, the ATVA and AMA busy themselves with impending legislation at the local, state, and federal levels regarding OHV recreation. They fight for the laws, rules, and regulations that they feel will most benefit their members and the industry as a whole. Contact the AMA at 13515 Yarmouth Drive, Pickerington, Ohio 43147, or call (800) AMA-JOIN, or check the organization's website: www.ama-cycle.org.

The BlueRibbon Coalition (BRC) is a membership-based organization dedicated to recreational land-access issues throughout the country. The group has often been described as the "pitbull" branch of OHV advocacy groups as it regularly engages in lawsuits against the anti-recreation access groups, which attempt to shut down and impede public motorized trail systems. The BRC also serves an educational role, its most recent being a program to quiet noisy dirt bikes and ATVs. BRC depends on the money derived from individual memberships to be able to fight its land-use battles. To join, contact the group at Blue Ribbon Membership, 4555 Burley Drive, Suite A, Pocatello, Idaho 83202, or call 1-800-BLUE-RIB (1-800-258-3742) or check out its website: www.sharetrails.org.

The National Off-Highway Vehicle Conservation Council (NOHVCC) is a multi-faceted organization that focuses primarily on "creating a positive future for off-highway vehicle recreation" by offering resources, documents, and educational materials to OHV enthusiasts and groups. One of the organization's initial goals was to form strong OHV state associations throughout the country so as to give it a unified voice in all political OHV matters. The organization also conducts workshops where land managers can communicate with OHV trail experts and enthusiasts. In addition, NOHVCC is dedicated to educational programs that deal primarily with the safety and ethics of OHV trail riding. NOHVCC is a nonmembership-based group that encourages riders to join an OHV club in their area. You can contact NOHVCC by calling (800) 348-6487, emailing trailhead@nohvcc.org or writing to 4718 S. Taylor Drive, Sheboygan, Wisconsin 53081. You can also find more about the organization's many services at this website: www.nohvcc.org.

"Twenty years from now you will be more disappointed by the things that you didn't do than by the ones you did do. So throw off the bowlines. Sail away from the safe harbor. Catch the trade winds in your sails. Explore. Dream. Discover."
— Mark Twain

state riding organizations, or as local clubs—we have a strong, unified voice that the movers and shakers in our communities tend to listen to.

So all right, that's one very important reason to join a club. However, there are many more. ATV clubs also are always planning weekend trips with groups of people, which nearly always makes the riding experience more fun. Even during the off-season, many ATV club members have occasional get-togethers just for the heck of it. There's even the aspect of having a huge pool of off-highway information from the club members, such as which aftermarket parts work best for your quad, who makes the best trailer, and what's the latest hot setup for pickups and RVs.

ARE CLUB RIDERS HAPPIER RIDERS?

From my experience with literally hundreds of ATV riders over the

Riding is one thing, but the main reason most folks go ATVing is to hang out with friends and family. Joining a club can enhance that part of experience tremendously.

"Get action. Seize the moment. Man was never intended to become an oyster."
— Theodore Roosevelt

One of the greatest things about ATV riding is that it allows us to get further into the backcountry in one day than we could in several days of hiking. Be sure to stop now and then and enjoy the great wilderness you have ventured into.

TIP

PLAN AN ENTIRE VACATION AROUND AN ATV JAMBOREE

Even if everyone in your family is not a rider, many of the ATV jamborees and festivals are located in parts of the country where there are plenty of other activities close at hand. Do a little research ahead of time to find out what's available in the area for the nonriders in the family.

---

years, I've found that the riders who are involved in local clubs tend to get the most satisfaction from their riding experiences. There is, however, a little of the old chicken and the egg question here—do riders who are really crazy about their sport tend to join clubs, or are they drawn even further into the sport by joining one? I imagine the answer is it's a little of both, but I do feel certain about one thing. Though I don't have any statistics to back me up, from what I've seen over the years, ATV riders who are active in their clubs

definitely seem to go riding more often, have more fun and more friends, and make an extremely positive impact on the future of *their* sport by always practicing and preaching impeccable off-highway ethics.

ISN'T MORE WORK INVOLVED?

OK, all the fun stuff about being a club member does involve a bit of work if you want to reap all of the benefits. Sure, someone has to be secretary, treasurer, and president, and someone has to make the campground

HAVE A BLAST AT ATV FESTIVALS AND JAMBOREES
ANNUAL GET TOGETHERS KEEP GETTING BIGGER

A phenomenon sweeping the ATV world over the past decade has been the increasing popularity of ATV festivals and jamborees. There are a variety of events now, some lasting over the weekend while others have family-fun activities for nearly a whole week. The following is a list of some of the more established events in North America and the general time of the year they are held (a contact phone number and website are also listed and be aware that this information is subject to change):

• **Mountain State ATV and Dirt Bike Jamboree**, usually held in late April in Boone County, West Virginia. For more information: (800) 592-2217; www.trailsheaven.com

• **Spring Jam**, usually held in late April in Perry Sound, Ontario. For more information: (705) 342-7582; www.springjam.ca

• **Vanderhoof ATV Jamboree**, usually held in late April in Vanderhoof, British Columbia. For more information: (250) 567-5567; www.vanjam.quads.ca

• **Iron County Memorial Weekend ATV Rally**, usually held in late May in Hurley, Wisconsin. For more information: (715) 561-4334; www.hurleywi.com

• **National ATV Jamboree**, usually held in mid-June in Fillmore, Utah. For more information: (800) 441-4ATV; www.mooracing.com

• **Dirt Days on the Hatfield/McCoy Trail**, usually held in mid-June in Logan County, West Virginia. For more information: (800) 592-2217; www.trailsheaven.com

• **High Mountain ATV Jamboree**, usually held in mid-July in Wallace, Idaho. For more information: (208) 556-4308; www.high-mountainatv.org

• **Oregon Dune Fest**, usually held in late July in Winchester Bay, Oregon. Information: (541) 271-3495; www.dunefest.com National ATV and Dirt Bike Rally Week, usually held in early

• **September in Wyoming County**, West Virginia. For more information: (800) 592-2217; www.trailsheaven.com

• **United States ATV Jamboree**, usually held in early September in Greeneville, Tennessee. For more information: (423) 323-5497; www.atvjamboree.com

• **Arapeen ATV Jamboree**, usually held in early September in Ferron, Utah. For more information: (435) 381-2493; www.arapeenatvjam.org

• **Arizona ATV Outlaw Trail Jamboree**, usually held in early September in Springerville, Arizona. For more information: (866) 409-9378; wwwazatvoutlawtrail.com

• **Rocky Mountain ATV Jamboree**, usually held in late September in Richfield, Utah. For more information: (877) 473-8368; www.atvjam.com

• **San Juan Safari**, usually held in late September in Monticello, Utah. For more information: (435) 587-ATV5; www.sanjuansafari.com

• **Hatfield/McCoy Trailfest**, usually held in late October in Mingo County, West Virginia. For more information: (800) 592-2217; www.trailsheaven.com

reservations and be in charge of signup, etc., but with a large group working together as one it's probably no more time consuming than planning a big trip for your family all by yourself. And to keep your trails open, there will probably be trail cleaning and trail maintenance days, and auction fundraisers or carwashes, but hey, those usually turn into real fun family activities.

STARTING A CLUB STEP-BY-STEP

So now that you're ready to join an existing club, or start one on your own, where do you begin? Well, there just happens to be an organization that will do everything in its power to help you in this quest, and it will do it all for free. The National Off-Highway Vehicle Conservation Council (also known as NOHVCC) has a stated goal of "creating a positive future for off-highway vehicle recreation." At the very top of its list is the task of getting as many riders as possible to join or form clubs. Why is this? Because the organization understands what a big boost every single member is for the future of our sport. (Plus, I guess, down deep, they just plain want you to have more fun!)

Joining an already established club is the easiest route. Virtually every state has a NOHVCC representative who has a master of list of all the dirt bike and ATV clubs in his or her state with phone numbers and e-mail contacts. To find the club nearest to where you live, simply call NOHVCC at 800-348-6487 and someone will get you hooked up with your state rep. There's also a list of the clubs on the website www.nohvc.org.

Of course, not all of us will be fortunate enough to have an established club ready to take us in for $20–$30 a year. In that case, you and your riding pals may want to start your own club from scratch. NOHVCC is also prepared to help you with that task, by offering a proven, and well-used, off-highway vehicle club start-up kit through the mail (once again, free). In it,

In some parts of the country, old railroad beds have been converted into trail systems. While many are limited to hikers and cyclists, some communities have opened up their "rails to trails" to ATVs and dirt bikes.

TIP

BE CAREFUL WHAT YOU NAME YOUR CLUB!

One of the best things an ATV club can accomplish is portraying a positive image to the local community. That's of utmost importance when it comes to keeping trails open and building new ones. In other words, in the eyes of the general public, OHV recreationists should be seen as responsible, family-oriented caretakers of our outdoor lands. We can begin this process by thinking twice about how we're going to name our ATV clubs. The Jackson County Dirt Diggers, Green Valley Stump Jumpers, or Birmingham Mud Hogs ain't gonna get the job done. Try something more like the Jackson County ATV Trail Riders, Green Valley OHV Explorers, or the Birmingham ATV Club. Not nearly as exciting, but you'll probably find more opportunities to ride!

you'll find easy-to-understand, step-by-step instructions on how to get your club up and running, as well as tips on maintaining a strong volunteer infrastructure, which is the key to the more successful and long-lived clubs.

CLUB START-UP RUNDOWN

In the NOHVCC off-highway vehicle club start-up kit, you'll find all the details on how to accomplish the following steps to getting your own club up and running:

• Getting the word out about your first meeting.
• Setting an agenda for the first meeting, which includes making introductions, sparking discussions, recruiting nominations/volunteers, identifying positions that need to be filled, identifying member's talents that can be utilized, education, and enjoying refreshments and social time.
• Setting an agenda for the first board of directors meeting, which includes discussing

job descriptions, dues, legal issues, insurance, and bylaws.

• Parliamentary procedures.
• Volunteer time records.
• Putting together a newsletter.
• Procedures for cash disbursements and receipts.

If all this sounds a bit intimidating, no need to worry because you'll also have personal access to your own state NOHVCC rep who is available to help you throughout the entire process if you happen to hit any snags. Eventually, of course, your state ATV club will want your new organization under its umbrella as well, which means by then you will have accomplished a job well done.

FEDERAL DOLLARS FOR TRAILS

Back in 1991 something happened in Washington D.C. that turned out to be a big plus for off-highway recreation. First proposed by Senator Steve Symms of Idaho and known as the Symms Act, this legislation advocated that a portion of federal gas tax money should go to off-road users (this was after a lot of hard work by OHV activist groups, including the BlueRibbon Coalition). The rationale behind it was common sense: If gas taxes were being used to build highways for cars and trucks, why shouldn't off-highway riders get their share (they're buying the same fuel after all!) of the taxes to pay for trail projects?

ATV clubs are not only a fun social function for their members, but they also allow them to speak with one voice when it comes to local trail access. One of the best ways to get more trail opportunities in your area is to join a club and work together with local land managers on getting more quality ride areas and trails built.

Many OHV land managers welcome volunteers for trail projects. Having the OHV community put a good foot forward in this manner certainly helps when land managers have to make decisions on motorized trail access.

TIP

GPS WORKS GREAT ON LONG ATV ADVENTURES

Global Positioning Systems (GPS) has changed navigation forever. Many GPS receivers exist, and they are now much easier to understand. You don't have to be a rocket scientist to figure them out. You can download way-points through the internet or from a CD, and the GPS will bring you right to your point of destination.

When you are purchasing a GPS for use on an ATV, it must be waterproof and it should have a plug that lets you connect it to the accessory outlet on your ATV. If you cannot plug your GPS in the outlet, you should bring many extra batteries with you since they burn batteries at an alarming rate, especially if the backlight is opened a lot.

The Symms Act passed and became law, much to the delight of the motorcycle and ATV world. There was a slight catch, however. A percentage of the funds would have to be used for nonmotorized trail projects as well, but none of us ATV enthusiasts were complaining.

Now almost 15 years later, there are dozens of ORV trail success stories thanks to the millions of dollars dispersed through the Symms Act. All-new ride areas have opened, as well as many established ones being saved and revitalized. Most of this occurred because of the efforts of the off-highway community, even though hikers, equestrians, mountain bikers, and cross-country skiers have benefited greatly as well.

The trouble is that when it comes to handing out millions of dollars, the government has to make sure the right folks are getting it and that the job will be done. So it's not easy as filling out a form and sending it in to wait for a check to arrive! The task of procuring Recreational Trail Program (RTP) funds can at first appear quite daunting, but there are a group of experts whose job it is to help you along the way. Most of the off-highway successes have been through group efforts such as state and local riding clubs, where you have more than one person taking on the task.

Your main source for information on the RTP is found on the web at www.fhwa.dot.gov /environment/rtpstate.htm. This provides a complete list of RTP state contacts. Your next step would be to contact the National Off-Highway Vehicle Conservation Council (NOHVCC) to get the name of your NOHVCC state representative, who may assist throughout the entire process. Contact NOHVCC at 800-348-6487 or email trailhead@nohvcc.org or check its website: www.nohvcc.org.

There are only a few places in the United States where legal ride areas exist along the coastline, most notably Pismo Dunes in central California and the Oregon sand dunes near the town of Winchester.

Index

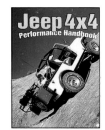
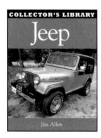

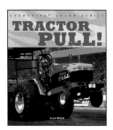